50
GREATS

CHELTENHAM TOWN
FOOTBALL CLUB

STADIA

50
GREATS

CHELTENHAM TOWN
FOOTBALL CLUB

JON PALMER & TOM GOOLD

Acknowledgements

We would like to thank the following people for their contributions:

Paul Baker, Paul Godfrey, Carol and Keith Palmer, Ian Mean, Anthony Thompson (ATP-photo.com), Murry Toms, Jamie Victory, *The Gloucestershire Echo* and *The Citizen*, Holly Bennion, Rob Sharman and Lucy Chowns at Tempus Publishing, Barrie Wood.

Jon Palmer and Tom Goold
September 2006

First published 2006

STADIA is an imprint of
Tempus Publishing Limited
The Mill, Brimscombe Port,
Stroud, Gloucestershire, GL5 2QG
www.tempus-publishing.com

© Jon Palmer & Tom Goold, 2006

The right of Jon Palmer & Tom Goold to be identified
as the Authors of this work has been asserted in accordance
with the Copyrights, Designs and Patents Act 1988.

British Library Cataloguing in Publication Data.
A catalogue record for this book is available from the British Library.

ISBN 0 7524 4150 7

Typesetting and origination by Tempus Publishing Limited.
Printed in Great Britain.

Foreword by Paul Baker

When Jon asked me to write a foreword for his new book I was delighted to accept. As a celebration of some of the great players that have graced Whaddon Road his timing could not have been better, with the team currently playing at the highest level it has ever achieved. I hope my short contribution does both Jon and the players he has chosen justice.

Jon, I know, has supported Cheltenham Town for a long time, long before the heady successes of the late 1990s when the number of regular supporters surged from at best 1,000 to 3,000 and more.

Many of those, including myself, who watched the team in the late sixties and beyond still do so today, and will doubtless recall fond memories as they read the book. I can think of no better qualified person to write this book than Jon, and incidentally no better person to cover our football club for the *Gloucestershire Echo*.

I am sure that the book will generate a lot of interest and debate amongst Cheltenham Town fans, in particular about who is in and who Jon has left out! It cannot have been easy to limit the number of 'greats' to fifty given our long history going back over 100 years.

Some of my fondest memories go back to the late sixties and early seventies when I first began watching the team. I still remember waiting after the game to collect autographs from my 'greats' at the time, players like Joe Gadston, Gerald Horlick, Dave Meeson, Roger Thorndale, Alan Jefferies and Pat Casey. Who can forget that fantastic goal scored by Dave Lewis against Banbury United one snowy midweek evening, a diving header when not only did the ball fly into the net but Dave followed, gracefully like a seal sliding on ice!

A little later I remember an energetic midfielder called Terry Paterson, a distinguished centre forward in Dylan Evans and the stylish Dave Dangerfield. I remember too some of my connections from school, my Economics teacher Julian Lailey and fellow pupil Kieron Hehir. There was also a certain Steve Cotterill who I remember playing against for NatWest versus Stretton United one Sunday morning; we lost 10-1 and he scored a few!

Jumping a few years I have great memories of the likes of Jimmy Smith, Jason Eaton and Lee Howells, not to mention our rock solid defensive partnership of Chris Banks and Mark 'Boka' Freeman; the silky skills of Clive Walker; the 'legend' Neil Grayson; that great finisher Dale Watkins; the little and large partnership of Julian Alsop and Tony Naylor; Michael Duff, our Northern Ireland international, and Jamie Victory, who remains a great ambassador for the club.

The danger of naming names is that the more you name the more you think of and the more you have to leave out. With the exception of Jamie I have deliberately chosen not to mention any of the current squad, all of whom are establishing their own bit of history with Cheltenham Town. Some, I am sure, will appear in the next edition. So it's over to you Jon – I'm looking forward to a great read.

Foreword by Jamie Victory

How do we define the word legend in football terminology? Whether it is over a long or short period of time, an achievement can be reached and a success story can be created. One goal or one game can determine the path a player or club takes.

Having dropped out of the professional game, I had an understanding and naivety that the quality of football and players in non-League would not be of a high standard, but I was proven wrong.

In my very first game for Cheltenham Town, playing with former professionals like Chris Banks, Lee Howells, Jimmy Smith and Mark Freeman, I could see the quality in abundance. It was obvious that some of these players were under-achieving and could play at a higher level.

My thoughts were to be realised as we rose through the leagues to gain Football League status for the first time in the club's history. With the core of the team from the non-League days performing well, we narrowly missed out on the play-offs by one point in our first season.

I am fortunate enough to have played with a large number of the players in this book, many of whom, like myself, have enjoyed successful spells with the club. Together they have helped Cheltenham Town achieve, and have been involved in, the club's mesmeric rise.

The most important word for me is 'togetherness' when I think about the players and the teams which have had success at Cheltenham. For me, without the close-knit team spirit, heart and endeavour, success would have been harder to reach.

When times are hard you look for people to be strong, not just physically but mentally, and that is a big factor in any sport, not just football. When I look at the list of players in this book, I have seen that in every single one of them. Their effort, skill and diverse attributes have contributed to our success and they fully deserve this accolade.

It is an honour and privilege for me to be included in this list and to be regarded as a Cheltenham Town 'legend'.

This fantastic experience in my life will always stay with me and one thing for sure is that I can say I have played a part in the history of Cheltenham Town Football Club.

Cheltenham Town FC 50 Greats

Julian Alsop
Brett Angell
Chris Banks
Ray Baverstock
Bob Bloomer
Steve Book
Mark Boyland
Steve Brooks
Mark Buckland
Chris Burns
Pat Casey
Peter Cleland
Paul Collicutt
Dave Dangerfield
Martin Devaney
Michael Duff
Jason Eaton
John Finnigan
Mark Freeman
Joe Gadston
Peter Goring
Bill Gourlay
Andy Gray
Neil Grayson
Gerald Horlick

Lee Howells
Brian Hughes
Joe Hyde
Alan Jefferies
Nick Jordan
Dave Lewis
Grant McCann
Jeff Miles
Russell Milton
John Murphy
Tony Naylor
David Norton
Ronnie Radford
Roy Shiner
Jimmy Smith
Paul Tester
Martin Thomas
Roger Thorndale
Jamie Victory
Anton Vircavs
Clive Walker
Tim Ward
Dale Watkins
Kevin Willetts
Mark Yates

G iant striker Julian Alsop holds the record for the most goals scored by a Cheltenham Town player during a single Football League campaign. The 6ft 5ins Alsop is also second only to Martin Devaney on the Robins' all-time Football League goals list, with 35 in his three seasons at the club. It was Alsop's prolific partnership with the diminutive Tony Naylor that lifted Cheltenham to their first promotion to League One at the end of the groundbreaking 2001/02 season.

A late entrant to professional football at the age of twenty-three, Alsop was born in Nuneaton on 28 May 1973. A former labourer and demolition worker, Alsop was given the chance to take up football as a profession after a successful spell with Southern League Premier Division club Halesowen Town. He had earlier played non-League football for Nuneaton, VS Rugby, RC Warwick and Tamworth. He scored a two-minute hat-trick for Tamworth

against Armitage during the 1994/95 season. He also appeared for Halesowen in a 2-1 defeat by Cheltenham at Whaddon Road during the 1996/97 season that was Steve Cotterill's first win as Robins' boss.

His form alerted Bristol Rovers, who paid the Yeltz £15,000 for his services in February 1997. He scored 4 goals in 20 League starts for Rovers, but struggled to hold down a first team place in his second season. He was loaned to Swansea City and after five appearances for the Welsh club, he signed permanently for £30,000 in March 1998. He scored the quickest ever hat-trick by a Swansea player when he netted three times in as many minutes in a Welsh Cup tie against Cwmbran. He helped Swansea win the League Two championship at the end of the 1999/00 season, but after 16 goals in 90 League appearances for the Swans, he departed on a Bosman free transfer in June 2000.

Alsop was on the verge of signing for Brighton and Hove Albion, but after visiting Whaddon Road and being shown around by Cotterill he was talked into signing for the Robins by the very persuasive manager; 'He was very professional and wouldn't let me go,' Alsop recalled. He made his Cheltenham debut as a substitute in a 2-2 opening-day draw with Mansfield Town on 12 August 2000. He made his first start a week later, partnering Neil Grayson in attack as Cheltenham won 2-0 at York City.

Alsop played alone up front at Watford in a League Cup first round tie and was excellent, only missing out on his first Robins goal by inches at Vicarage Road, but he was sent off a week later in a 2-0 win over Torquay United at Whaddon Road. He broke his duck in a 2-0 win at Hull City, a win that put Cheltenham on top of the Football League's bottom division for the first time. He scored in a 2-1 defeat at Macclesfield Town, before registering his first brace for Cheltenham in a thrilling 4-3 home win over Tony Cottee's Barnet at Whaddon Road. He scored against Shrewsbury Town in a 4-1 FA Cup success, and in the 3-1 win over eventual champions Brighton, which was one of the highlights of the season for Cheltenham. Often ploughing a lone furrow in attack, Alsop managed 5 League goals in 29 appearances during his first season at Cheltenham, but he showed a dramatic improvement in the following campaign.

During his first season at the club he didn't feel as though he had properly settled in Cheltenham. He was living with his mum in the Midlands, or staying at his house in Swansea and spent large chunks of the season travelling to and from Cheltenham. His opportunities were also restricted by the form of Grayson, who had finished as Robins' top scorer for three years in succession. But a change of accommodation and two additions to the Cheltenham playing staff lifted Alsop. Naylor was brought in from Port Vale and wide player Lee Williams was recruited from Mansfield, and they both formed deadly combinations with the target man. Alsop also moved in with Robins teammate Jamie Victory, along with new signing Keith Hill, who cooked the majority of his meals! When Hill was loaned out to Wrexham, Alsop met his future wife Kathryn Hamblin and he was firmly settled in Cheltenham.

On the pitch Williams' crosses from the right flank and Naylor's trickery and intelligence in attack gave Alsop a new lease of life. His best run of form came in February and March when he scored 6 goals in 5 matches. He scored League braces against Mansfield Town, Exeter City and York City. It was not all plain sailing for Alsop though. Earlier in the campaign he returned to play against his former club, Swansea, and helped Cheltenham earn a point after a 2-2 draw; however, he suffered a bang to his eye which badly bruised the retina. He was advised not to play for at least three months or run the risk of losing his eyesight, but he battled on, encouraged by his manager, and thankfully he had no further problems with his eyes.

Alsop also played a major part in the record breaking FA Cup run that saw Cheltenham reach the fifth round for the first time in their history. He scored twice against Kettering Town in the 6-1 first round win and a diving header against Hinckley in round two. His finest cup moment came against Burnley when he headed home Russell Milton's cross to give Cheltenham a 2-0 lead against Championship club Burnley in the fourth round, and the Robins progressed with a 2-1 win.

He scored a total of 26 goals during the 2001/02 season and was named as Supporters' Player of the Year at the end of Cheltenham's third promotion success in six seasons. He was slimmer and sharper during his second season and his most important strike was against Rushden and Diamonds in the 3-1 play-off final triumph at the Millennium Stadium. He was watched by over fifty friends and family for the biggest game of his career and he didn't let them down, scoring the all-important second goal to put Cheltenham ahead after Rushden had cancelled out Martin Devaney's opener.

Alsop described the 2001/02 season as the best of his career and handed some of the credit for his goalscoring exploits to his girlfriend,

Julian Alsop (left) in action with Cardiff City's Danny Gabbidon in the League One 1-1 draw at Whaddon Road on 31 August 2002.

as well as Naylor and Williams. Alsop believes that Naylor was the best player to represent Cheltenham Town in his time at the club, describing his partner in crime as being in a 'different class'; 'We didn't really work on it, we just turned up and hit it off,' Alsop said of his deadly partnership. He also lists Steve Book as the finest goalkeeper that he has played with, ranking the Robins favourite above Roger Freestone of Swansea and Andy Collett of Bristol Rovers. 'A massive authority who had the respect of the lads' is how Alsop described Cotterill, the manager who utilised his height and power to the best effect.

Cheltenham went up to League One and Alsop did not match the heights of the previous year, but he still finished as top scorer for the second season running with 12 goals in all competitions. He hit the winner against Brentford in a 1-0 home success, but was sent off amid ugly scenes after going on as a substitute in the return match at Griffin Park. He was present virtually throughout the season, missing only a handful of matches through illness. However, his contract expired at the end of the 2002/03 season and despite a last-ditch contract offer from Bobby Gould, he signed for Oxford United on a free transfer; 'We were too old and the squad was

not big enough,' Alsop said of the relegation season. His final goal for Cheltenham came in a 1-1 home draw against Luton Town and his last appearance was as a substitute in the 1-0 defeat at Notts County that confirmed the Robins' relegation. He scored 5 goals in 29 appearances during his first season at the Kassam Stadium, but his second year ended in controversy when he was sacked for a training ground incident.

Alsop signed for Northampton Town, but switched to Forest Green Rovers after seven appearances for the Cobblers. He moved to Rovers' Conference rivals Tamworth, but returned to Nailsworth during the 2005/06 season. He helped Forest Green avoid relegation, before moving on to Conference South club Newport County, where he was reunited with his former Robins colleague John Brough. He scored on his debut for the Welsh club in a 3-3 draw at Fisher Athletic, where Brough was also on the scoresheet. Alsop is still in regular contact with many of his former Robins teammates and played in Jamie Victory's testimonial match in July 2006, representing the Legends XI.

Marlborough-born Brett Angell was signed for Cheltenham Town by John Murphy as a raw nineteen-year-old in 1987 after spending two years on the books at Portsmouth. He had impressed Murphy while playing in a six-a-side tournament, and the Robins boss converted him from a central defender to a striker. Angell responded by scoring 25 goals in 39 games to kick-start his career before moving to top flight club Derby County, managed by Arthur Cox, for £45,000 in February 1988.

His finest moment in a Cheltenham Town shirt came at Molineux on 14 November 1987, where he gave the Robins a shock early lead in the FA Cup first round tie against Wolverhampton Wanderers, before Steve Bull scored a hat-trick to bring Cheltenham back down to earth and earn Wolves a 5-1 passage into the second round. His first Cheltenham

goal had arrived against Altrincham in a 1-0 win on 31 August 1987. He scored in the Robins' next two outings, at Kettering Town and against Welling United at Whaddon Road. He failed to find the net in the following match against Telford United, but scored a hat-trick against Dorchester Town in the FA Cup first qualifying round, giving him 6 goals in 5 matches. He scored in a 2-2 draw against Wycombe Wanderers on 23 September and netted the winner against Weston-super-Mare in the FA Cup second qualifying round 2-1 victory. Angell scored a consolation goal for Cheltenham as they were hammered 5-1 against eventual champions Lincoln City and he scored a brace the following week as Cheltenham bounced back with a 2-0 win over Fisher Athletic. His final goal came in a 5-3 defeat at Wycombe Wanderers on 16 January 1988, and his final appearance was a 2-1 win over Bromsgrove Rovers on Valentine's Day.

After leaving Cheltenham for the Football League, Angell found first-team opportunities hard to come by at the old Baseball Ground and, eight months later, Stockport County boss Asa Hartford splashed out a then-club-record fee of £33,000 to bring Angell to Edgeley Park in October 1988. Angell made his Hatters debut in a 1-1 draw at Scarborough and scored his first goal a week later when Hartlepool were beaten 3-0 at Edgeley Park. The arrival of Danny Bergara as the new manager of Stockport triggered a vast improvement in Angell's goalscoring form.

Five games into the 1989/90 season, Hartlepool were beaten 6-0 at Edgeley Park, with Angell hitting four of the goals. He was the first County player to score four goals in a match for more than two decades. Angell went on to find the net 23 times in 43 starts that season as Stockport enjoyed their finest campaign for over twenty years, but they missed promotion by a solitary point.

Angell won the golden boot for topping the Division Four scoring charts before asking for a transfer. He agreed a move to Southend, the club that had pipped Stockport to promotion.

A tribunal set the transfer fee at £100,000, with £19,500 going to Derby as a sell-on. Southend finished as runners-up to Cambridge United to win a place in the old Division Two for the first time in their history.

Angell continued to score goals at the higher level, prompting speculation of a move to the top flight. Everton swooped to sign the striker for £500,000 in January 1994. He played with the likes of Duncan Ferguson, Anders Limpar and Vinny Samways during his spell at Goodison Park. Angell only managed 1 goal in 20 appearances for the Toffees, but the Merseysiders sold him for £600,000 to Sunderland in March 1995. Things did not go well for Angell on Wearside and he fell out of favour and was loaned to Sheffield United, West Bromwich Albion and Stockport, before returning to Stockport on a permanent basis in November 1996.

Stockport reached the fourth round of the FA Cup, the semi-finals of the Coca-Cola Cup, the area finals of the Autoglass Trophy and promotion to English football's second tier for the first time during a memorable 1996/97 season. Angell confirmed his place in County's history by scoring the goal that secured promotion at Chesterfield in a 1-0 win. By the time Angell brought his second spell at Edgeley Park to an end, he had netted 95 goals and only Jack Connor, Kevin Francis and Alf Lythgoe have scored more. Angell finished top scorer at the end of each of his four full seasons at Stockport and was inducted into the club's hall of fame in 2002.

Another highlight for Angell came in 2000/01 when he helped Walsall win promotion to what is now the Championship via the play-offs. He appeared against Cheltenham during a loan spell at Port Vale and also for QPR, who beat Cheltenham 4-1 at Loftus Road. He also came up against Cheltenham for Rushden and Diamonds as a substitute in the 2001/02 play-off final at Cardiff's Millennium Stadium, as Steve Cotterill's Robins won 3-1 to claim a place in the third tier of English football for the first time.

Brett Angell shows the form that earned him a £45,000 move to Derby County in 1988.

Cotterill had earlier approached Angell about a return to Whaddon Road, but it never materialised and after fifteen years as a professional, Angell retired in 2004. Angell's brother Darren also played for Cheltenham during the 1987/88 season, scoring twice in 14 appearances before joining Lincoln City. During a distinguished professional career, Brett represented thirteen clubs and scored over 200 goals in more than 540 appearances in the full-time ranks. His career was taken full circle when he was employed as a youth team coach at Portsmouth in 2005, but he was relieved of his position in April 2006 after five months in the role.

Chris Banks

Defender, 1994-2003

Long-serving club captain Chris Banks called time on his professional playing career in 2003 after nine glorious years at Cheltenham Town. He decided to take the advice of a surgeon who had said that his knee could no longer cope with the rigours of full-time training. He was a great servant to the club and his Cheltenham career was one long success story.

Banks was signed for a tribunal-set fee of £10,000 by Lindsay Parsons in July 1994. Parsons had been trying to sign Banks for some time before he finally secured a deal. Banks had started out at Port Vale as a trainee, signing professional terms in December 1982. He operated at full-back in those days and went on to make 65 first team appearances for the Vale Park outfit, including their shock FA Cup win over Tottenham. He also managed one Football League goal; something which he repeated at his next club Exeter City and also for Cheltenham Town. Banks joined Exeter in the close season of 1988 and stayed at St James' Park for one

year, making 48 starts. He joined Conference side Bath City the following summer and spent five seasons at Twerton Park.

Banks made his first appearance for Cheltenham in a 2-1 friendly win over Oxford United. He went on to make 397 starts for the club, with a further four substitute appearances. His competitive debut was at Rushden and Diamonds' Nene Park in the Southern League Premier Division. Cheltenham won 2-0 that day and it soon became obvious that Banks was a class apart. He went on to make 54 appearances that season as Cheltenham finished as runners-up to Hednesford Town, setting a new club points record of 86 in the process. Banks found the net twice in his first season; at home to Sittingbourne with a spectacular diving header, and away to Sudbury in a 5-1 victory. He formed a formidable central defensive partnership with Steve Jones, who was to earn a move to the professional ranks with Swansea City. Banks won the Supporters' Player of the Year award in his first season and the Robins won the County Cup to give Banks a taste for lifting silverware. He was to do this on a regular basis throughout his time at the club.

Banks took over from the departing Neil Smith as club captain for the 1995/96 season. In what was very much a transitional season for the club, Banks made 50 appearances and found the net on 5 occasions. November saw Banks' partner Steve Jones leave for the Vetch Field and Banks found himself alongside the likes of Nick Dunphy and Dave Read in the centre of defence, before new boss Chris Robinson made a signing that would lead to arguably the finest defensive duo Cheltenham have ever had. Robinson paid £7,500 to Gloucester City for the services of towering centre half Mark Freeman. Banks and 'Boka', as he was universally known, first played together in a 0-0 draw against Freeman's former club, Gloucester. Their second game together also resulted in a clean sheet for Cheltenham and this was to set the trend for the rest of their partnership together. Cheltenham eventually finished third behind Rushden and Halesowen Town in the League.

There was optimism around Whaddon Road at the start of the 1996/97 season; the rebuilding had been done and it was time to earn that elusive promotion to the Conference. The season began with Banks alongside Freeman, but Robinson soon brought centre half Garry Wotton into the side and Banks was pushed forward into midfield. He began his spell there with 3 goals in 2 games. He scored at Gravesend & Northfleet in a 3-1 win and then hit his only brace for Cheltenham, putting two past Atherstone at Whaddon Road the following Tuesday. At that level, Banks could have easily played as a winger; he always had time on the ball and looked a cut above with the ball at his feet. He returned to the defence as the Robins enjoyed a fine run in the FA Cup. They were beaten in a first round proper replay by Barry Fry's second division Peterborough.

Cheltenham's league form became erratic and Gresley Rovers pulled away at the top of the table. Defeats at the hands of Dulwich Hamlet in the FA Trophy First Round and at home to Forest Green Rovers in the Dr Marten's Cup spelt the end for Chris Robinson, and Steve Cotterill took over at the helm. Banks was influential as Cheltenham edged out local rivals Gloucester City to win promotion to the Conference on a nail-biting last day at Burton Albion's Eton Park. Banks made 52 appearances along with another 5 goals to add to his tally and Cheltenham were back where they belonged. What was to follow for Banks and Cheltenham was the stuff that dreams are made of. Speaking in March 2002, Banks recalled how he had no idea what the club was capable of achieving when he joined back in 1994: 'They had just come down from the Conference and, in my mind, they had always been a Conference club, so it was just a case of getting them back where they belonged. As for the success in the Conference and beyond, it's been unbelievable,' he said.

After five frustrating years trying to gain promotion back to the Conference, Cheltenham, led by Steve Cotterill, took the top echelon of non-League by storm. Banks was a key figure during

Chris Banks 'guest stars' for Aston Villa during his benefit match in 2000.

the 1997/98 campaign as Cheltenham surpassed their previous best season by a considerable margin. An unforgettable FA Cup run saw the Robins reach the Third Round for the first time since the 1933/34 season. They eventually bowed out to Championship side Reading after a replay.

On a proud March night for Banks and for Cheltenham Town in general, he made his England Semi-Professional international debut at Crawley's Broadfield Stadium against Holland. He was joined by Cheltenham team mates Lee Howells, Dale Watkins, Jamie Victory and Neil Grayson. Banks shone at centre half alongside Stevenage's Mark Smith in the 2-1 win for England and it established Banks as one of the non-League game's leading defenders.

Banks made 57 starts that season and was awarded the Supporters' Player of the Year award for the second time. Cheltenham finished second in the Conference behind Halifax and, on 17 May 1998, Banks' proudest moment arrived; Cheltenham won the FA Trophy at Wembley Stadium, defeating Southport 1-0 with a goal from Jason Eaton. Banks made his way up the famous steps to pick up the Trophy and spark scenes of wild celebration.

Banks scored Cheltenham's first goal of the 1998/99 season at Welling, but Cheltenham went on to lose 2-1. It was then back to business as usual for Banks, alongside Freeman, as Cheltenham put together a run of seven consecutive wins to press their claims for the title after many thought Rushden were set to run away with it. After a spell on the sidelines with an Achilles injury, Banks returned to help guide the Robins to the title. He had missed the previous two visits to Rushden's Nene Park which had both ended in 4-1 defeats. However, this time he was prominent as Cheltenham snatched that unforgettable 2-1 win to put themselves in pole position for the Championship. Banks also played a crucial role in the Robins' thrilling title-winning victory over Yeovil at Whaddon Road. Banks, who made 45 starts that season, raised the Conference Championship Trophy. The reality set in that Cheltenham Town would be playing in the Football League for the first time in their 107-year history. At the age of thirty-three, Banks would be returning to full-time football after a ten-season absence.

Before Cheltenham officially left non-League football, Banks had time to make his second appearance for England in the 2-1 win over Wales at Clarence Park, St Albans. He would have had more caps to add to his two, but missed out through his troublesome achilles.

Banks made the step up to Division Three look rather easy, just as he had done with the step up from Southern League to Conference. He made his Football League debut for Cheltenham in the 2-0 opening day defeat at the hands of Rochdale. Cheltenham struggled in the opening weeks, but Cheltenham soon found their feet at their new level and began to make a charge towards the play-offs.

He was rewarded for his loyal service to Cheltenham Town with a benefit match against Aston Villa at Whaddon Road. Villa had all their stars on show with Benito Carbone, David James, Dion Dublin, Gareth Southgate et al. There was a great atmosphere and Villa, who were preparing for their FA Cup final against Chelsea, put on a superb show to win 7-1. Banks even turned out for Villa in the second half and it was a night to remember for him and everyone concerned with Cheltenham Town.

Back in the League, a remarkable turnaround in form meant that Cotterill's side needed a win at Southend on the final day of the regular season to guarantee a place in the play-offs. However, it was not to be and Hartlepool stole the final play-off position as Southend came from behind to win 2-1. It was an admirable effort from Cheltenham in their maiden season in the League and Banks was revelling in his second chance in the full-time ranks. Banks made 41 starts in League Two and 48 in total and he was now looking firmly towards a long-awaited return to League One where he had previously played for Port Vale.

Cheltenham missed out on the play-offs again at the end of the 2000/01 season after a nightmare run of injuries, but Banks was in his usual assured form and won the Players' Player of the Year award for his efforts. He made 46 starts in total to maintain his remarkably consistent form for Cheltenham and he scored his first Football League goal for eleven years in the 1-1 draw at Kidderminster.

The 2001/02 season was to be yet another memorable one for Banks and Cheltenham as the success story continued. After a disappointing start, Cheltenham recovered and with Banks forming another impressive partnership with Michael Duff, they were serious contenders for automatic promotion. Unfortunately, Banks missed out on the glorious run-in through injury, but he played his part in his side's best ever FA Cup run. Banks played in rounds one to five as Cheltenham made it to the last sixteen for the first time in their history. He was outstanding in the shock 2-1 win over high-flying Division One side, Burnley,

Former England defender Gareth Southgate presents Chris Banks with a framed Aston Villa shirt at his benefit game.

in round four. Banks then kept Jason Roberts quiet in the 1-0 fifth round defeat against West Brom in front of over 27,000 at the Hawthorns. On 26 March 2002, Banks limped off in the 2-1 home win over Kidderminster and was forced to sit out the rest of the season. Cheltenham went on to win promotion by beating old foes Rushden 3-1 at the Millennium Stadium in the play-off final. Banks joined in the post-match celebrations and was rightly allowed to hold the trophy aloft along with skipper on the day Mark Yates. Banks' career had gone full circle

– from League One to League One via the Southern League, Conference and League Two – but what a journey it had been.

Banks would undoubtedly be one of the first names on any all-time Cheltenham Town XI. He was at the centre of the club's rise from obscurity and few would argue with Cotterill's description of Banks as probably the best signing the club has ever made. He was a great servant to the club and a great role model on and off the field.

Long-serving and versatile, Ray Baverstock, or 'Baver' as he was commonly known, was named as Cheltenham Town's Player of the Year at the end of the 1987/88 campaign.

Baverstock's career began at Swindon Town, where he served as an apprentice before signing professionally in December 1981. He made his league debut for Swindon in a 2-1 defeat at Blackpool nine months later. He contested a first-team place with Charlie Henry at the County Ground and helped the Wiltshire Robins reach the FA Cup fourth round in 1982/83. Swindon beat Wealdstone, Brentford and Aldershot (7-0) to earn the right to face Burnley in round four, where they succumbed 3-1. Baverstock made 19 first-team appearances for Swindon, playing in the same side as Brian Hughes and Martin Blackler before Alan Wood swooped to sign him for Cheltenham in July 1983.

A tough tackling midfielder or defender,

Baverstock was Cheltenham's leading marksman during the 1983/84 season with 13 goals in League and cup from his 40 appearances. He made his debut against Sutton Coldfield Town on 20 August 1983 and scored his first goal against Hastings United in a 2-0 on 10 September.

The highly competitive Baverstock was influential as the Robins won the Southern League Premier Division title for the first time in 1985 and reached the FA Trophy quarter-finals, also for the first time in 1985/86. He played in 48 of the matches during Cheltenham's title winning campaign of 1984/85 and scored 11 goals, as they clinched the championship from runners-up King's Lynn with a final day win over Alvechurch.

Baverstock played against Maidstone United in Cheltenham's first ever Conference match, which they won 2-1 thanks to goals from Steve Brooks and Brian Hughes. He made 53 appearances during the debut season and scored 2 goals to take his Robins career total to 26 in 153 outings.

He featured in the 1986/87 FA Trophy third round tie against Kidderminster Harriers, which was watched by 3,567 spectators and he made 44 appearances during his fourth season with the club, adding another 2 goals to his tally.

Baverstock helped Cheltenham equal their best Trophy run with another last eight appearance in 1987/88, but their Wembley dream was ended in a 4-2 defeat at the hands of Telford United in front of 3,157 fans at Whaddon Road. He appeared for Cheltenham in the FA Cup first round tie at Molineux, where the Robins took a shock lead through Brett Angell, but finally succumbed 5-1 to Wolverhampton Wanderers. He made 52 appearances and scored 2 goals during the 1987/88 season.

Baverstock finished with 31 goals in 325 outings and was rewarded for his loyal service with a joint testimonial match against Everton in April 1990, which Cheltenham won 1-0 with Neville Southall guest starring in the Robins goal. His final competitive appearance came on the last day of the 1989/90 season at Kidderminster Harriers,

Ray Baverstock (right) shows his competitive style for the Robins.

where Cheltenham won 2-1 courtesy of goals from Richard Crowley and Kevin Willetts. Baverstock made the short move to Gloucester City three months later and played in the Tigers side that finished as Southern League Premier Division runners-up to Farnborough at the end of the 1990/91 season.

Spells at Worcester City, Bath City, Moreton Town, and another stint at Gloucester followed before he signed for Trowbridge Town in July 1993. Twelve months later, Baverstock returned to Gloucestershire with Forest Green Rovers, but he took over as Cirencester Town's player-boss three months later. He guided the Centurions to the Hellenic League and Cup double in 1995/96 as Cirencester took their place in the Southern League. Baverstock never gave anything less than 100 per cent for Cheltenham and his never-say-die attitude endeared him to the Whaddon Road faithful.

Bob Bloomer

Defender/midfield, 1992-2001

Bob Bloomer makes a trademark crunching tackle in a Southern League match.

There have been few more popular goals at Whaddon Road in recent years than Bob Bloomer's sixteenth and final strike for Cheltenham Town against Brighton and Hove Albion in February 2001. Bloomer had not scored a League goal since 1997 when he crashed in a wonder goal against eventual champions Halifax Town. But with Cheltenham winning 2-1 against the promotion-bound Seagulls, he went on as a sixty-fourth-minute substitute and stole the show. Six minutes after going on, he picked the ball up, advanced towards the Brighton box and curled a delightful shot into the far left corner bringing the house down and sparking a joyous lap of honour. Bloomer's playing career was coming to an end, but he was already established as one of the club's great servants and it was a wonderful note on which to bow out. He made three further substitute appearances and his last outing in a Robins shirt came against Southend in a 2-1 victory on 5 May 2001.

Robert Stephen Bloomer played a major part in Cheltenham's rapid rise from the Southern League to the Football League and he is still a popular and highly respected figure at the club, these days looking after the youth and reserve teams at Whaddon Road.

Bloomer was born on 21 June 1966 in Sheffield and is a passionate supporter of Wednesday. He played for the Owls' nursery sides as a boy, but it was when he was turning out for Sheffield Sunday League side Harrow United that he began to attract the attention of professional clubs. He was subsequently offered a trial by Chesterfield and signed professional forms at the age of eighteen. He spent the following five years at Saltergate, making 141 League appearances and scoring 15 goals. He made his Football League debut against AFC Bournemouth in 1986 and was made captain of the Spireites at the age of twenty-three. But in March 1990, Bristol Rovers paid £20,000 for his services. He spent two years with the Pirates, making 22 League appearances before embarking on a seven-year spell in non-League football with Cheltenham.

Bob became a fixture in the Robins line-up during the 1992/93 campaign, making his debut at Chelmsford in a 1-1 draw in August 1992. After suffering a serious knee tendon injury during his Gas days, Bloomer broke his leg at Corby in the 1994/95 season. He battled back to fitness and became assist-ant manager to Chris Robinson and then player-coach during the reign of Steve Cotterill. He played at full-back during his early seasons at Whaddon Road, but was converted into a combative all-action midfielder. The versatile Bloomer actually appeared all over the pitch for Cheltenham, including emergency goalkeeper. He played alongside Lee Howells in the centre of Cheltenham's midfield in the FA Trophy final success against Southport at Wembley. It was Bloomer's brave lunging block that denied Southport captain Brian Butler a clear goalscoring opportunity during the first half and helped preserve Cheltenham's clean sheet on the hallowed Wembley turf. A year later, Bloomer was an integral part of the Conference title-winning side that lifted Cheltenham into the Football League. He played in the opening day defeat at Welling United and then missed the following eight games with a calf muscle injury. He had returned to his all-action self by Christmas and made a total of 42 appearances in all competitions during the championship campaign. His only goal came against Bristol City in a 3-2 County Cup semi-final victory.

Bloomer (right) during his days as a full-back.

In 1999, Bloomer was a professional footballer again at the age of thirty-three after two and a half years as a fitness instructor. He played in Cheltenham's first match as a League club against Rochdale, but spent much of the next two seasons on the bench. He was awarded a richly deserved benefit match against his old club Bristol Rovers before his final campaign, which Cheltenham won 2-1. He was called upon during the 2000/01 season during an injury crisis and he filled in wherever needed. He played particularly well in the goalless draw at Watford in the League Cup first round first leg at Vicarage Road. Bloomer retired after making 267 appearances for the Robins in three different divisions.

As well as being a wholehearted and talented player, he has always been a hugely popular character at Whaddon Road and long may his association with the club continue. Bloomer oversaw a successful 2005/06 season for Cheltenham's reserve team that saw them win the Pontins Holidays Combinations Wales and West Division. They also reached the finals of the League Cup and the Gloucestershire County Cup, where they were beaten by Colchester United and defending champions Yate Town respectively. Bloomer's boys claimed some deserved silverware to commemorate their impressive campaign, when they defeated Premiership club Reading's second string 2-1 at Whaddon Road in the Championship play-off in August 2006. Steve Gillespie scored both of the Robins' goals and it was a very youthful and talented side that took to the field, underlining the potential waiting in the wings for first-team opportunities at Cheltenham.

Steve Book
Goalkeeper, 1997-2004

Steve Book was Cheltenham Town's number one as they became the surprise package in the Conference during the 1997/98 season and he went on to enjoy unprecedented success during his seven-year spell at the club.

Book junior followed in his father Kim's footsteps. Kim played for Bristol Rovers, AFC Bournemouth, Northampton Town, Doncaster Rovers and Bath City. His uncle Tony was also a distinguished professional with Plymouth Argyle and, more notably, Manchester City, who he captained and managed. While he was at Northampton, George Best famously put six goals past Kim Book for Manchester United in an FA Cup tie.

Steve's career started out at Western League club Welton Rovers and he also turned out for Weston-super-Mare and Frome Town before he was given a chance in professional football with Brighton and Hove Albion. He spent a summer taking part in pre-season training with

the Seagulls and he was told that he would be given a full-time contract by manager Barry Lloyd. But Lloyd, who managed Brighton from 1987 to 1993, resigned two days later and new boss Liam Brady released Book.

He moved on to Lincoln City, where the hard-up club were unwilling to take a chance on a young goalkeeper unproven at Football League level. After two knock-backs, Book moved to Forest Green Rovers, where chairman Trevor Horsley and manager Frank Gregan were in the process of transforming the Nailsworth club's fortunes. Book picked up a Southern League Southern Division championship medal at the end of his first season at The Lawn and appeared at Whaddon Road against Cheltenham in Rovers' 1-0 Dr Marten's Cup win just before Steve Cotterill took over from Chris Robinson as Robins manager.

Cotterill was looking for a goalkeeper the following summer as Cheltenham returned to the Conference after a five-year absence. He paid Rovers £8,000 for Book and it turned out to be one of the best signings the club ever made. Things did not get off to the best of starts for Book; Cheltenham were beaten 3-0 by Dover Athletic on his debut at The Crabble Athletic Ground on 16 August 1997. Cheltenham won their next two matches against Hayes and Woking at Whaddon Road, but Book's costly error at Hereford gave the Bulls a 3-2 win. However, Book's form improved after he kept his first clean sheet at Kettering Town, five days after his Hereford nightmare, and he began to fulfil Cotterill's prophecy that he would become the top goalkeeper in the Conference. He played in all 42 Conference matches as Cheltenham finished second behind Halifax Town. They also reached the third round of the FA Cup for the first time since 1933/34. Book featured in every match of the FA Cup run as Cheltenham beat Thatcham Town, Merthyr Tydfil, Paulton Rovers and Sutton United to reach the first round proper where they knocked out Tiverton Town 2-1. Cotterill's team beat Boreham Wood 2-0 in a second round replay to book a place in round three where they took old Division One club Reading to a memorable replay in front of a sold-out Whaddon Road.

Book had arguably the best back four ever to represent Cheltenham in front of him in the shape of Michael Duff, Chris Banks, Mark Freeman and Jamie Victory. As well as their historic Cup run, Cheltenham progressed to the FA Trophy final for the first time and Book played in every round as Cheltenham breezed past Enfield, Rushden and Diamonds, Ashton United, Hayes and Dover Athletic to reach Wembley, where they would face Conference rivals Southport. The Sandgrounders were the better side on the day, but Book made a match-changing save from Brian Ross as Cheltenham won the Trophy thanks to Jason Eaton's seventy-ninth minute winner. Bournemouth-born Book played 60 of Cheltenham's 61 matches that season, missing one County Cup tie against Bristol City. His form for Cheltenham earned him an England Semi-Professional call-up and he represented his country in Holland and against England, Wales and a Highland League XI on home soil.

His good form continued as Cheltenham went one better than their runners-up finish in 1997/98 to win the Conference and gain promotion to the Football League in 1999. One of the highlights of Book's season was a breathtaking save from Kidderminster Harriers skipper Mark Yates, who would sign for Cheltenham later in the campaign. Cheltenham won the match at Aggborough 1-0 on their way to the title.

Book turned professional as Cheltenham took their place in the Football League and his kicking and handling improved noticeably with full-time training. He played in the club's first League match against Rochdale in 7 August 1999, which ended in a 2-0 defeat. Cheltenham missed out on the play-offs narrowly at the end of their first season in Division Three, but Book's consistent record continued as he appeared in all 46 League matches. He repeated that feat a year later as Cheltenham finished ninth, two places outside of the play-off spots. He was given the Nationwide Save

of the Month award for a spectacular stop at Hull City, where Cheltenham won 2-0 to top the division for the first time early on in the 2000/01 campaign.

He sustained an injury during the summer of 2001 and missed the first six matches of the 2001/02 season. Cheltenham failed to win any of the six matches, but Book returned in a 2-0 win over Carlisle United and the Robins enjoyed the finest season in their history to finish fourth, missing out on automatic promotion on the final day of the season at Plymouth. Book always produced the goods in the biggest matches and

Steve Book displays excellent handling against Carlisle United in a 2-0 League Two win on 15 September 2001.

he was excellent in the play-off semi-final win over Hartlepool which Cheltenham won on penalties. He also had a solid game in the final as Rushden and Diamonds were defeated 3-1 and Cheltenham were celebrating their third promotion in six seasons.

He played in 36 of Cheltenham's 46 Division Two matches, but for the first time in his Robins career he faced serious competition from Shane Higgs, who had been his deputy for the previous three seasons without forcing his way into the first team. Cheltenham were relegated on the final day of the season and Book started the 2003/04 season back in the basement division

as first choice goalkeeper, but he only made five appearances and his cause was not helped by a dismissal at Boston United.

Book was released in the summer of 2004 and spent a year with Swindon Town, where he was second choice to Rhys Evans. He made two league appearances for Swindon, but was released after one year at the County Ground. He signed for Cirencester Town in the summer of 2005, but joined Bristol Rovers where he was installed as goalkeeping coach and back-up to regular number one Scott Shearer. Book, now thirty-seven, was released by Rovers at the end of the 2005/06 season.

A bubbly and likeable character, Book endeared himself to the Whaddon Road faithful with his outstanding goalkeeping and interaction with the songs from the terraces. He was often seen to be conducting the chants at away games as Cheltenham attacked in search of a goal at the other end. Book made 172 Football League appearances for Cheltenham and played 316 matches in total for the Robins along with 1 substitute appearance.

Widely regarded as one of Cheltenham's best ever forwards, Mark Boyland was the leading scorer in the Robins' Southern League championship triumph in 1984/85 and also scored 8 goals in 21 appearances for Wycombe Wanderers.

Swindon-born Boyland started his career at Oxford City before moving to Banbury United in July 1979, where he was leading marksman in his first season. He played alongside future Northern Ireland international Kevin Wilson during his spell at Banbury.

Following a brief period at Witney United, Boyland signed for John Murphy's Cheltenham in August 1984. He made his debut in a 1-1 draw against Gravesend and Northfleet on the opening day of the 1984/85 season. His first goals came against Folkestone Town, when he scored a hat-trick in a 4-1 win on 1 September 1984. He scored against Bideford in an FA Cup first qualifying round triumph and netted a brace against Bromsgrove Rovers in a 2-0 Southern League Cup victory. The goals continued to flow and he fired four goals against Dorchester Town in an FA Trophy third qualifying round win in Dorset which the Robins won 5-1. He scored another treble against AP Leamington in a 6-0 league win and his third and most important hat-trick of his debut season came against Gloucester City on 30 April 1985 as Cheltenham charged towards the title. He made 58 appearances and scored 31 goals during his memorable first season at Whaddon Road as Cheltenham won the championship by two points from runners-up King's Lynn.

Boyland was a true master of holding the ball up with his back to goal and topped the scoring charts again as Cheltenham reached the FA Trophy quarter-finals for the first time in 1985/86 and took their place among non-League's elite clubs in the Conference. He scored 22 goals during his second campaign at the club, including five braces, to give him an impressive 53 goals in his first two seasons with the Robins.

Talented and a great entertainer, Boyland scored in the high profile Trophy third round tie against rivals Kidderminster Harriers in 1986/87 which was watched by a Whaddon Road crowd of 3,567; but the Robins were beaten 3-2 by their Worcestershire rivals. He scored 23 goals in 49 appearances that season, including hat-tricks against Willenhall Town and Dagenham in a 6-1 win. Steve Cotterill was one of Cheltenham's other scorers that day and Cotterill, who was to become a hugely successful manager of the club, later hailed Boyland as the top striker he saw turn out for the Robins during his playing days.

Boyland scored 5 goals in 18 appearances during the first four months of the 1987/88 season, before making the move to Wycombe for £10,000 in November 1987. The final goals of his first spell at Cheltenham came against Wealdstone in a 4-1 win on November 17, when he scored twice. He scored twice on his Chairboys debut at home to Boston United and he also netted a spectacular thirty-yard winner at Runcorn. He scored against his former Robins teammates a week later, but Cheltenham progressed in the FA Trophy after a thrilling 3-2 first round win thanks to a brace from Mark Buckland and one from Steve Brooks. Wycombe avenged their defeat a month later in the Conference, with Boyland also on target in another highly entertaining 5-3 win. Boyland followed up his goals against Cheltenham with a hat-trick against Macclesfield Town in February 1988. During his spell in Buckinghamshire, Boyland played alongside one-time Robins trio Martin Blackler, Steve Abbley and Martin Woodall. In total, Boyland scored 8 goals in 20 Conference outings for Wycombe. He moved to Aylesbury United in October 1988 and briefly partnered record goalscorer Cliff Hercules in attack for the Ducks.

Boyland returned to Whaddon Road in March 1989 for £7,000 and he announced his return with four goals in a 4-1 win at Chorley and scored 8 goals in 13 appearances in the final

two months of the 1988/89 season. He made 26 appearances and scored 10 goals during the 1989/90 season leaving him with a Robins career total of 99 goals in 220 appearances. He left Cheltenham again in July 1990, this time for VS Rugby, whom he helped finish third in the Southern League Premier Division in 1992. He made another brief return to Cheltenham at the start of the 1992/93 season when Cheltenham had suffered relegation to the Southern League. He scored his 100th Robins goal against Weymouth in a 2-2 draw at Whaddon Road on 25 August 1992 after going on as a substitute. He scored one more goal against Worcester City which proved to be his final appearance for the Robins.

After 101 goals in 224 outings, he signed for Worcester in January 1993 prior to spells with Gloucester City, Tamworth and Cirencester Town, whom he joined in July 1994. He spent some time as assistant boss to his old Robins teammate Ray Baverstock, with Martin Blackler (player-coach) and Steve Abbley (chairman) also part of the ex-Cheltenham contingent at the Centurions.

Boyland is one of only five players to reach a century of goals for the Robins, the others being Dave Lewis, Gerald Horlick, Jimmy Smith and Jason Eaton. He now runs his own kitchen fitting company in Banbury.

Steve Brooks was one of the stars of Cheltenham's first spell in the Conference and the stylish midfielder was a key member of the Robins engine room for seven seasons. Hugely talented on the ball and blessed with tremendous balance and vision, Brooks was the creator of many a Cheltenham goal. His career was cruelly cut short by a knee injury in 1992, but he was rewarded for his highly entertaining spell at the club with a testimonial match against Manchester City in August 1994.

Brooks was born in Woodstock, Oxfordshire on 14 July 1961 and started his footballing life with Marlborough Comprehensive School. He caught the attention of Coventry City while playing Hellenic League football for Clanfield, but signed for Witney Town in 1980. After recovering from a broken ankle, Brooks scored 29 goals and was voted Witney's Player of the Year in his second season at the club. Reading offered Brooks a trial and he played in two friendlies for the Royals against Wantage and Oxford United. He was approached by the Football League club, but opted to remain in part-time football due to his work as a successful electrician and his family commitments. He stayed at Witney for five years, scoring 113 goals in 260 matches from midfield. Brooks had always impressed in matches against the Robins and when financial issues forced Witney to release some of their players, Cheltenham boss John Murphy was quick to snap up the highly rated playmaker.

He signed for Cheltenham in July 1985 and made his debut in the Southern League Championship match against cup winners Fisher Athletic on 18 August 1985. He scored Cheltenham's first ever Conference goal in the opening league match against Maidstone United in a 2-1 win one week later. Brian Hughes scored Cheltenham's other goal that day. He made 53 appearances during his first season at Whaddon Road and scored an impressive 15 goals as Cheltenham finished their first season of Conference football in eleventh place. He went on to captain the club for four of the following seven campaigns and was called up to the England Semi-Professional squad in 1988. He was the first Robin to win non-League international recognition and considered his call-up to be the highlight of his career. He made his England debut against Wales as a substitute at Rhyl, winning two further caps.

Brooks made 50 appearances during the 1986/97 season and scored 5 goals as Cheltenham finished eleventh once again. He played in a fine 3-1 win at Scarborough when Cheltenham became one of only two teams to beat the eventual champions on their own ground that season. He scored at Maidstone United in a creditable 1-1 draw in Kent and was also on the scoresheet in a 1-1 draw at defending champions Enfield, who finished fourth that season.

He played in the big FA Cup first round tie at Wolverhampton Wanderers the following season, making 52 appearances and scoring 14 goals in the 1987/88 campaign. He converted a penalty in the first qualifying round win over

Steve Brooks (right) shows his poise on the ball.

Dorchester Town, when Brett Angell scored a hat-trick in the 4-1 success.

Brooks made 38 appearances during the 1988/89 season, adding a further 4 goals to his total to give him career Cheltenham figures of 38 goals in 193 outings at the end of his fourth season.

He maintained his consistent record during the 1989/90 season with 48 appearances and 9 goals as Cheltenham finished eleventh in the Conference for the third time in five seasons. Brooks appeared against Birmingham City in the FA Cup first round tie in November 1990, which Cheltenham lost 1-0 at St Andrews. He scored four goals that season and at the end of the campaign he had played 268 times for the club.

His final season saw Cheltenham suffer demotion from the Conference after seven years at the highest level of non-League football. Brooks made his last appearance against Welling United on 2 May 1992, when a 3-2 win was not enough to prevent relegation. He made a total of 310 appearances and scored 56 goals for the club before his knee problems finally got the better of him.

At the end of the 1991/92 season, Cheltenham took on an Aston Villa XI containing several first team stars. During the first half a far from fit Brooks stood out and impressed the Villa coaching staff watching from the dugouts. Despite almost constant interest from League and other Conference clubs, Brooks remained loyal to Cheltenham and he possessed set piece expertise and dribbling skills to rival any player who has played for the Robins.

Mark Buckland

Defender/midfield, 1979-1982, 1987-1992

managed by Graham Allner at the time. He joined fellow former Robins Graham MacKenzie, Malcolm Kavanagh and Alan Ollis, and starred for the Brakes as they won the Southern League title in 1982/83. They were eighteen points behind Kidderminster Harriers at Christmas, but went on an amazing run in the second half of the season. Buckland scored 14 goals from right-back and his performances soon began to attract the attention of the big clubs.

He made a dream move into the professional ranks with Wolverhampton Wanderers in February 1984, where he made 50 appearances in the top flight and old Division Two. He was persuaded to sign by manager Graham Hawkins and made his debut against Burnley after the usual Wolves right-back had picked up an injury. Buckland scored ten minutes into his debut and he went on to make 17 appearances that season, playing against the mighty Manchester United at Old Trafford and taking on Tottenham Hotspur at White Hart Lane. He impressed with his work-rate as an attacking right-back at Molineux, but was released by the then-Wolves boss Tommy Docherty and was reunited with Allner at Kidderminster in the summer of 1985. He reached the Welsh Cup final while with the Aggborough club, but returned to his home town team in April 1987 after some persuasion from Dave Lewis and produced some of the best football of his career during his second spell at Cheltenham.

Buckland became a key figure in the Cheltenham side that reached the FA Trophy quarter-finals in 1987/88 and he also took on his former club Wolves in the first round of the FA Cup in the same season. He finished as the club's top scorer and Player of the Year for two consecutive seasons and played in virtually every position on the pitch. After 315 starts, with a further eighteen as a substitute, and 75 goals for the Robins, Buckland moved to Gloucester City in 1992 where he spent two seasons. He then enjoyed spells with Cirencester Town, Moreton Town and Endsleigh in the Hellenic League.

M ark Buckland began his Robins career at the age of eighteen and was a local lad in the truest sense as he was brought up just a stone's throw away from Cheltenham's Whaddon Road home. He scored twice on his debut in a 4-2 win over Enderby on 13 October 1979, after progressing through the youth and reserve sides. The week of his Cheltenham debut was a particularly memorable one for Buckland. He played for the youth team on the Saturday and scored two goals. He appeared for the reserves on the Tuesday and scored another brace. He then enjoyed his successful senior debut and was given the match ball to commemorate a remarkable week of football. A former Oakley School pupil, Buckland also gained County Youth honours and during his first spell in the Cheltenham senior side he registered 7 goals in 54 Southern League starts.

Buckland was then one of several Cheltenham players signed by AP Leamington, who were

Local-lad-made-good Mark Buckland celebrates a goal.

In a bizarre episode during the 1997/98 season, fans of Cheltenham Town were given one last chance to see their former hero in action. Cheltenham were playing Stevenage Borough in the Conference at Whaddon Road. After a bomb scare resulted in the ground being evacuated, the vast majority of the 2,580 crowd made their way over the nearby Whaddon Rec. Buckland was playing for Crescent United against Hardwicke, much to the delight of the Robins faithful, who chanted his name and cheered on the Northern Senior League side until they were allowed back into the ground over the road.

Buckland, a scaffolder by trade, is married to Yvonne and they have two children Rhea and Alec. He was one of the most versatile players ever to pull on the red and white of Cheltenham and his popularity at the club can be measured by his back-to-back Player of the Year awards.

Chris Burns
Midfield/defender, 1988-1991

Midfield hard-man Chris Burns is still playing semi-professional football at the age of thirty-eight in his role as player-manager of Southern League Division One Midlands outfit Cinderford Town.

Manchester-born Burns started out as a youth team player at Bristol City, but made his name at Cheltenham Town before progressing to the Football League to play for Portsmouth, Swansea City and Northampton Town. He played in Pompey's FA Cup semi-final against Liverpool in 1992, where the south coast club were agonisingly beaten on penalties after a replay at Villa Park had finished goalless. Burns also played in the original tie, which ended in a 1-1 draw at Highbury after Portsmouth had beaten Exeter City, Leyton Orient, Middlesbrough and Nottingham Forest to book their place in the last four.

He joined Cheltenham from Sharpness in the summer of 1988 and made his debut in a 3-2 defeat at Weymouth on 23 August. He made 41 appearances during his first season at Cheltenham but failed to find the net. That changed dramatically during the 1989/90 campaign, when Burns scored an astonishing five goals in a 6-0 Midland Floodlit Cup match against Alvechurch at Whaddon Road on 12 December 1989. He had not scored in 59 previous Robins appearances, many of which saw him playing at left-back, but he demonstrated his attacking potential with his five-goal salvo. He had scored 131 goals from 26 matches playing for Matson in the Gloucester Youth League so always knew he was capable of finding the target! He scored again eight days later in a 3-1 defeat at Stafford Rangers, but it was his ball-winning ability and highly competitive and combative style that caught the eye.

Burns made a total of 31 appearances during his second year at Cheltenham as the Robins finished eleventh in the Conference. He started the following season at Whaddon Road, but he was sold to Portsmouth for £20,000 in February 1991. He made a total of 108 appearances for the Robins and scored 13 goals, 7 during his final season with the club. He helped Cheltenham reach the first round of the FA Cup, scoring in the first qualifying round tie against Exmouth, as the Robins were held to two draws, but won the second replay 3-0. Cheltenham knocked out Weston-super-Mare, Worcester City and Dorking to earn a trip to Birmingham City's St Andrews in the first round proper. Burns and Cheltenham gave a brave account of themselves, but were beaten 1-0 by the old Division Three club. He made his final start against Macclesfield and scored the Robins' consolation goal in a 5-1 drubbing at Moss Rose.

The transfer came as a shock to the bricklayer, who was asked by his friend Allan Gough if he would like to spend a week training at Portsmouth as he couldn't work due to bad weather. Gough had been at Swindon Town at the same time as Frank Burrows, then Pompey's manager, and Burns decided to venture down to Hampshire to investigate how the full-timers set about it. He was asked by Burrows if he wanted to be a professional footballer and played in three practice matches. He played for the reserve team against the first team twice and was then asked to play in the first team against the reserves. At the end of the third match Burrows told Burns that he had already signed him and that he was a professional footballer.

It was during his first season that Burns found himself caught up amid the excitement of Portsmouth's Cup run. He also played at Old Trafford against a Manchester United team including Ryan Giggs, Bryan Robson, Gary Pallister and Steve Bruce. United won the League Cup third round tie 3-1. Jim Smith took over as manager at Fratton Park and was described by Burns as a 'father' to him and the other youngsters at the club at the time such as Darren Anderton, Kit Symons, Andy Awford and Daryll Powell. Burns made 109 appear-

Chris Burns in action for Cheltenham before his move into the professional ranks.

ances for Portsmouth before going on loan to Swansea City and AFC Bournemouth. More than 60 matches for Northampton Town later he left the full-time game with around 250 games under his belt and returned to semi-professional football at the age of twenty-eight.

He said that he wanted to finish his playing days with his friends and he returned home to play for Gloucester City before a spell with Forest Green Rovers in the Conference. He returned to Gloucester and took over as player-manager, building a team of local players, including talented youngsters Neil Griffiths, Tom Webb and Chris Thompson, from scratch, winning promotion to the Southern League Premier Division and reaching the FA Trophy quarter-finals. After five years in charge at Meadow Park, Burns resigned along with former Robins midfielder Keith Knight in January 2006 and the pair joined Cinderford Town as players.

Following the resignation of Cheltenham Town's Football in the Community Officer Mike Cook as manager of the Forest club, Burns took the reins as player-boss in July 2006 and away from football he works as a bricklayer in Gloucester.

Pat Casey
Striker, 1971-1978

Pat Casey will always be remembered in Cheltenham Town folklore as the man who created the majority of Dave Lewis' record 291 goals for the club, despite scoring 69 goals in 236 games for Cheltenham himself. Casey was eighteen when Bob Etheridge signed him from Stonehouse in 1971 after a recommendation by Robins' goalkeeper Geoff Pellant.

Casey made his debut against Ilkeston Town on the opening day of the 1971/72 campaign. He scored his first goal against Gloucester City and went on to score 15 goals in 40 appearances, including a purple patch of 6 goals in 5 games. He followed up his successful debut season with 12 goals in 42 appearances in his second campaign. Cheltenham finished third in the Southern League Division One North for the second season running. The Robins set a new club record of 18 Southern League matches undefeated, but a 1-0 home defeat to Atherstone on 21 April 1973 cost them promotion.

Casey was on target in Cheltenham's first two matches of the 1973/74 season, hitting the net in the 2-1 home win over Stevenage Athletic on 11 August 1973 and three days later in a 3-2 defeat at Banbury United. Cheltenham finished third for the third year running. Casey made 42 appearances and scored 15 goals, including a brace against Dunstable in a 4-1 win in April 1974. He missed the opening two matches of the 1974/75 season through injury, but returned to score 15 goals in 49 appearances as his strike partner Lewis racked up an incredible 53 goals in 56 games, setting a new club record. He sustained a horrendous broken leg at Merthyr Tydfil on 23 March 1976 after colliding with Merthyr goalkeeper Don Payne while chasing a through ball. Casey did recover and stayed at Cheltenham for another four years, but he was never quite the same player. His misfortune ended his 1975/76 campaign and he was restricted to five appearances the following season, when Cheltenham finished second in

the table to Worcester City and won promotion to the Premier Division. Casey scored 1 goal in 14 appearances during the 1977/78 season. His final outing came against Bedford Town as a substitute on 12 April 1978.

Casey spent four years as player-manager at Shortwood United and another four at Sharpness, before leaving to play for Leonard Stanley for two years. He returned to Shortwood for a second spell, winning the Hellenic League Premier Division title and the County FA Trophy, before being lured to Forest Green Rovers. When he took over at the Nailsworth club they were bottom of the Southern League Midland Division. Casey and his assistant John Evans guided Rovers to safety, but the pair were dismissed the following season when Trevor Horsley took over, appointed Frank Gregan, and trebled the playing budget. After his spell at Forest Green, Casey returned to Cheltenham and ran the reserve team during Chris Robinson's time as manager of the Robins. He departed when the club turned professional in 1999 and linked up with Doug Foxwell at newly formed Gloucester United.

Peter Cleland
Striker/midfield, 1954-1958

Peter Cleland was a centre forward or outside right who played for Motherwell in the Scottish League and Newarthill Hearts in Scottish Junior football before joining Cheltenham Town in October 1954 when his family moved to England. He was born on 8 May 1932 in Glasgow and had already been spotted in Scotland by Cheltenham manager Arch Anderson, who added him to his growing list of Scottish players at the club.

He was twenty-four years old when he made his debut for the Robins away to Chelmsford City in a 1-1 draw on 30 October 1954, having already appeared for the reserves in a Birmingham League match against Lye Town. Described as a fast and strong outside-right who was difficult to dispossess, Cleland later converted to play at centre forward after Anderson tried a series of high profile players in that position without lasting success. He scored his first goal for Cheltenham Town on 11 December 1954 in a 2-1 Southern League win at Dartford and went on to find the net in the next seven consecutive matches over the Christmas and New Year period. In all he scored 19 goals in 31 League and cup appearances as the Robins finished fourth in a strong Southern League that season.

The following campaign was even more successful with Cleland scoring 20 times in 47 League and cup starts as the team finished second in the League – their highest ever placing until the Southern League championship was finally won in 1985.

In season 1956/57 Cleland played in each tie as Cheltenham won through from the preliminary round to reach the first round proper of the FA Cup. He played in front of the record crowd at Whaddon Road – 8,326 – for the visit of Reading in November 1956. Cheltenham took the lead when Cleland headed a corner back across goal for Jimmy McAllister to score, but Reading came back strongly in the second half to win 2-1.

Despite finishing sixth in the table during season 1957/58, Cheltenham Town scored a club record 115 goals in 42 league matches and Cleland topped the scoring charts with 39 from 49 starts in all competitions. That season, Cheltenham scored nine goals on three separate occasions – against Kidderminster Harriers, Merthyr Tydfil and Guildford City – and

Cleland scored 8 goals across those 3 games. He also scored seven times in the Southern League Cup as Cheltenham reached the final and defeated Gravesend & Northfleet for their only success in the competition.

During the summer of 1958 Cleland was transferred to Norwich City, who were then in the Football League third division, and he spent two years with the Canaries before returning to Cheltenham Town in January 1960 for a brief spell before moving on to Southern League Bedford Town in October that year. In total he made 200 appearances for the Robins, scoring 109 goals.

Paul Collicut is presented with the Southern League Championship shield in 1985.

When Paul Collicutt was fifteen he was courted by Bristol City, Southampton and Queens Park Rangers and at the age of sixteen he signed full professional forms for Swindon Town. In between, he became the youngest player ever to appear for Cheltenham Town.

Collicutt led Bishop's Cleeve into the Southern League at the end of the 2005/06 season after the Kayte Lane club finished as runners-up to Didcot in the Hellenic League Premier Division. He started out at Cleeve Colts after moving to the area with his family from Shipston-on-Stour at the age of nine. He began playing football at Bishop's Cleeve Primary School. He joined Hester's Way Junior Colts, before the club changed its name to Cleeve Colts. He played in the same team as future Robins teammate Tim Bayliffe, who is now his assistant at Cleeve. They struggled at first, taking on teams with older players, but in their second season they did the League and cup double; a feat they repeated for the next three years. Collicutt also won the county schools' under-15 and under-16 titles and he was spotted by scouts from Bristol City while playing for the county team. He signed schoolboy forms for

Bristol City and he would play for his school team on a Saturday morning before getting a train from Cheltenham to Temple Meads and a bus to Ashton Gate to play for City in the afternoon. He'd return home in the evening and play the following day for Cleeve Colts.

After two years at Bristol City, Collicutt was disappointed not to be offered an apprenticeship. He left to join Cheltenham and played in the youth team and the reserve side that was managed by Roger Thorndale in the West Midlands League. He was named as a substitute for the first team at the age of fifteen against Witney Town on 27 December 1975. He made his full debut against Enderby Town in a 3-0 win on New Year's Day under boss Dennis Allen. He cemented his place in the starting line-up as Cheltenham went on a run of one defeat in eighteen matches. Collicutt operated in midfield, but chipped in with some valuable goals and his first senior strike arrived against King's Lynn in a 3-2 home win on 28 February 1976. He netted against the same opposition in the return fixture a week later in a 4-1 victory. He scored in a 3-3 draw with Banbury United in Oxfordshire and was on the scoresheet along with Dave Lewis in a 2-0 home win over Bromsgrove Rovers. He made 17 starts and scored 4 goals during his first season as Cheltenham finished fifth in Southern League Division One North.

Collicutt spent a week on trial at Southampton and QPR before joining Swindon. He was 'tapped up' by QPR's Frank Sibley, who took him to London and introduced him to former England international Stan Bowles and Dave Thomas. He spent a week there when Rangers were top of the first division and stayed in the same hotel as Phil Parkes, who had moved from West Ham to Loftus Road. He played in trial matches for Rangers, but he went to Southampton the summer after they had won the 1976 FA Cup with a 1-0 win in the final over Manchester United. He appeared for the Saints' reserves against the club's full FA Cup winning side and the second string claimed a 1-1 draw and Collicutt scored their goal. He was offered apprenticeship forms at Southampton and QPR, but Swindon's Danny Williams handed him a full-time contract.

After three years at Swindon, he returned to Cheltenham for a month. He spent a week on trial at Halifax Town, but was also tempted by an offer from non-League Trowbridge Town. He accepted the Wiltshire club's offer and began his career in senior non-League football. He was converted into a central defender by former Sheffield United striker Alan Birchenall and installed as club captain at Frome Road. Trowbridge finished third behind Alvechurch and Bedford Town in the Premier Division of the Southern League in 1980/81 and were promoted to the top division of the amateur game, then the Alliance Premier Division, because the other clubs were not considered suitable. Once again, Collicutt was attracting the attention of the big clubs, but he was sent off for the only time in his career playing against Corby Town in front of a West Ham United scout. Three years later, Collicutt returned to Cheltenham, who were managed by Alan Wood at the time. During the next eighteen months, Cheltenham went up to the Conference and Trowbridge were relegated.

Collicutt played 48 matches in Cheltenham's Southern League Premier Division-winning campaign and scored 3 goals. He played 20 games during the first season in the Conference, 34 matches during the 1986/87 season, making a total of 175 appearances for the Robins and scoring 8 goals. He went on to play for Gloucester City, Forest Green Rovers, Newport County, Cinderford Town and Evesham United.

He was assistant to John Evans at Forest Green and then to Frank Gregan and he was the man who recommended former Cheltenham Town and Forest Green player Steve Jones to Swansea City in 1995. Collicutt has taken Cleeve into the Southern League for the first time in their history and helped develop Kayte Lane into a ground of which the club can be proud. The Skinners, as they are nicknamed, made national headlines by reaching the fourth qualifying round of the FA Cup during the 2005/06 season. They were narrowly beaten by Eastbourne Borough after beating Corsham Town, Bideford, Fairford Town and AFC Totton during the club's best run in the competition. Collicutt has carved out a successful career in non-League management and he runs a thriving meat business away from football. It will always remain a mystery how a player of such talent never played in the Football League.

Dave Dangerfield
Defender/midfield, 1973-1980

Dave Dangerfield joined Cheltenham Town in 1973 and made his debut in a 1-0 Southern League Division One win at Merthyr Tydfil on 27 October. He signed initially on loan from Charlton Athletic, having also played in the Football League for Swindon Town. The Stroud-based left-footer stayed at Whaddon Road for six seasons and became known as a versatile player who filled in at full-back or midfield.

A former England Schools international, he won seven caps for his country at under-15s level before Swindon snapped him up. He was apprenticed at fifteen and was given his senior debut against Tranmere Rovers in the old Division Three by Swindon boss Dave Mackay. He appeared against Arsenal in the third round of the FA Cup at the County Ground, where the Wiltshire Robins were beaten 2-0.

He was struggling to break into the Swindon side the following year and Mackay left his post

as boss with Les Allen taking over. Dangerfield was one of several players released by Allen at the end of the 1972/73 season and spent three months with Charlton. He suffered from an achilles tendon problem, which affected him on hard ground for the remainder of his career.

Dangerfield was signed by his old Swindon teammate Willie Penman, who was in charge at Whaddon Road between 1973 and 1974. During his first season, he made 31 appearances and scored 4 goals, including a fine treble in a 3-2 win over Kidderminster Harriers at Whaddon Road. His other goal came in a 2-1 triumph at King's Lynn and Cheltenham finished third for the third year running in Division One North of the Southern League.

He made 51 appearances during the 1974/75 season, contributing 9 goals, with 36 appearances and 3 goals the following season. He was an important member of the side which won promotion to the Southern League Premier Division in 1976/77, making 49 appearances and scoring 4 goals as Cheltenham finished as runners-up to Worcester City.

He made a total of 316 appearances and scored 27 goals before treading the well-worn path to Gloucester City at the end of the 1979/80 season. His final appearance was at Minehead in a 2-0 defeat on 3 May 1980 and he was undoubtedly one of the most talented players in the line-up throughout his time as a Robin.

After joining City, Dangerfield moved to Forest Green Rovers in the Hellenic League. It was at Forest Green that he enjoyed some of his most memorable days. He played at Wembley in the 1982 FA Vase final as Rovers beat Rainworth Miners' Welfare 3-0. It was the finest day in the Nailsworth club's history and despite only appearing for ten minutes as a substitute it was Dangerfield's fondest memory. He remained at Forest Green for their first season in the Southern League and then moved on to Shortwood United.

Martin Devaney
Winger/striker, 1999-2005

A Young Martin Devaney dreams of a successful career in professional football.

Former Balcarras school pupil Martin Devaney is currently Cheltenham's leading Football League marksman with 38 goals in 203 league outings during his six seasons at Whaddon Road. Cheltenham-born Devaney was an exciting and pacy winger, who could operate on either flank or up front and he was named as Player of the Year at the end of the club's first season in League One. He started his career at local youth teams such as FC Lakeside and Charlton Rovers as well as winning a host of representative recognition, including Republic of Ireland youth honours.

At the age of thirteen, Devaney's precocious talent was spotted by Birmingham City, who signed him on schoolboy forms and he stayed at St Andrews for the remaining two years of his school days. He was offered a place on the Blues' Youth Training Scheme, but he was lured to Coventry City, who were then in the Premiership.

Devaney spent the next three years at Highfield Road and signed a professional contract at the end of his first season as a Coventry trainee. He played in the Sky Blues' youth and reserve sides, appearing alongside the likes of Dion Dublin and Darren Huckerby, but he was released by Coventry at the end of the 1998/99 season and arrived at Whaddon Road for pre-season training the summer before Cheltenham's first year in the Football League.

He made his debut as a substitute on the opening day of the 1999/2000 season as Cheltenham's historic first Football League outing ended in a 2-0 defeat at home to Rochdale. Devaney was called up to the starting line-up for the second game of the campaign against Norwich City in the League

Cup as Cheltenham gave an excellent account of themselves at Carrow Road. He retained his place for the trip to Mansfield the following weekend and he appeared on the left wing as Neil Grayson's header earned Cheltenham their first Football League goal and win at Field Mill.

His season was interrupted by a broken foot which he sustained in a reserve team match. He was sidelined for two months, but returned in the New Year and scored his first goal in a 1-1 draw at Hull City's former home, Boothferry Park. He scored his second goal two weeks later at Barnet in a 3-2 defeat and demonstrated that he was a capable striker as well as having obvious flair from wide positions.

Devaney finished his first season at Cheltenham with 6 goals in 26 League appearances. The pick of his strikes was a memorable solo effort against Lincoln City in a 2-1 win at Sincil Bank. The

following season, Devaney became the first player to score a Football League hat-trick for Cheltenham, firing a treble against Plymouth Argyle in a 5-2 win at Whaddon Road in September 2000. He developed an uncanny knack of scoring against clubs from Devon, having scored twice against Torquay and once against Exeter City during his first season at Cheltenham. He followed up his three goals against Argyle, with a second half brace at Exeter the following week. Four weeks earlier he had also been on target for the second season running at Hull in a 2-0 win as Cheltenham topped the division for the first time early in the campaign. He finished his second season with ten goals, but found first-team opportunities hard to come by in the 2001/02 season.

Devaney started 8 of Cheltenham's 46 Division Three matches as they finished fourth

and faced Hartlepool in the play-offs. He had not started a League game since November 2001, but he was recalled for the first leg of the semi-final at Victoria Park which finished 1-1. He was back on the bench for the second leg, but with Russell Milton injured, Devaney was given a start in the Millennium Stadium final on the left of midfield. He scored the opening goal against Rushden and Diamonds and was later named as Man of the Match in the 3-1 triumph as Cheltenham reached the third tier of English football for the first time. Devaney thrived at the higher level and scored 6 League One goals in 35 starts. He also scored in the 2-0 FA Cup win over Yeovil Town, but Cheltenham were relegated on the final day of the season at Notts County.

He scored 5 goals in 32 starts as Cheltenham returned to League Two and finished fourteenth under John Ward, who took over from Bobby Gould in October 2003. The 2004/05 season proved to be Devaney's final campaign at Whaddon Road and he made 38 appearances, hitting 10 goals to top the scoring charts as Cheltenham finished fourteenth for the second successive season.

He exercised his right to move on as a free agent and was snapped up by Championship club Watford, but moved to Barnsley in August 2005, signing a two-year deal at Oakwell. Devaney scored eight goals for Andy Ritchie's team as they returned to the Championship with a play-off final triumph over Swansea City at the Millennium Stadium in May 2006.

Defender/midfield, 1996-2004

Michael Duff is undoubtedly one of the finest players ever to come through the youth system at Cheltenham Town. He also became the first player to earn full international honours while at the club when he made his Northern Ireland debut against Cyprus in February 2002.

Belfast-born Duff, now twenty-eight, is currently plying his trade at Coca-Cola Championship club Burnley, who he joined in a £30,000 deal during the summer of 2004. It was a little over ten years ago that a gangly looking youngster by the name of Duff first appeared for Cheltenham's reserve team after a recommendation from Carterton Town manager Derek Bragg to the club's then youth development officer Mike Davis.

Duff's father, John, is from Dublin and his mother, Marlene, is from Belfast. After being born in the Six Counties, he spent the early part of his life in the north-east of England. He spent some time as a schoolboy at Nottingham Forest before joining Darlington and he supported the Quakers as a youngster. When his family moved

south, he signed for Swindon Town youth, but he ended up at Carterton Town in the Hellenic League.

Robins manager Chris Robinson was looking at potential recruits for the club's Youth Training Scheme and sought the advice of Crewe Alexandra boss Dario Gradi. Gradi told Robinson to look out for the good players who were maybe a little tall for their age, perhaps a bit skinny or short. The big clubs would get all the best youngsters, but there was a chance that one such player would be a late developer once they had filled out or grown a few inches.

Soon after being given an opportunity to impress at Whaddon Road, it was obvious that Duff had a special talent. He had started only six games for the reserves before he made his debut as an eighteen-year-old on 24 September 1996 against Dorchester Town in a 1-1 draw. The Cheltenham team that day was: K. Maloy, M. Duff (M. Bellingham), J. Wring, G. Wotton, M. Freeman, J. Victory, D. Wright (L. Howells), C. Banks, J. Eaton, P. Chenoweth, B. Bloomer. Sub not used: D. Clarke. At the end of Duff's first season in the side at right-back, Cheltenham were promoted to the Conference after finishing as runners-up to Gresley Rovers and Duff was an established first-team player under new boss Steve Cotterill. He made 18 starts and 6 substitute appearances during the 1996/97 season.

A year later, young Duff was walking out on the hallowed turf of Wembley Stadium, as the Robins capped a wonderful campaign with an FA Trophy victory over Southport on 17 May 1998. He started 59 of Cheltenham's 61 matches during the groundbreaking 1997/98 campaign. There were always rumours around Whaddon Road that scouts were monitoring the progress of Duff and it seemed only a matter of time before he was offered a chance in the professional ranks. Thanks to Cheltenham's fantastic 1998/99 season, he was able to graduate from apprentice to pro with the Robins and he played a vital role in the Conference Championship success which earned Cotterill's men a place among the elite ninety-two clubs

that season, which he said helped him develop his game. Duff's first goal as a professional came against Exeter City in a 3-1 win on Boxing Day 1999.

It was not until Mark Freeman left the club in the summer of 2001, that Duff began to play regularly in the middle alongside captain Chris Banks. The duo first played as a central partnership at Southend in September 2001 and they formed an immediate understanding. Their partnership flourished until Banks sustained a knee injury that ultimately ended his career. Duff then played alongside John Brough and Richard Walker, partnering the latter in the play-off final triumph over Rushden & Diamonds at Cardiff's Millennium Stadium in May 2002.

Duff looked more than capable of playing at League One level, but Cheltenham struggled after making their third step up in five years and suffered an immediate return to League Two. Duff showed his versatility when he was used as a striker by boss Bobby Gould and scored 2 goals in 2 games as Cheltenham narrowly lost their battle against the drop. He remained at Cheltenham for one more season in the basement division, before he was snapped up by his former mentor Cotterill and given a chance to show off his defensive skills a league below the Premiership. Duff left Cheltenham with a host of honours and with 366 starting appearances, with 6 as a substitute, to his name. He scored 16 goals in total, 12 of which came during his 201 Football League appearances in the red and white.

He memorably appeared as a late substitute for Northern Ireland as Lawrie Sanchez's team famously defeated England in September last year. Once a raw youngster full of potential, Duff is now proving that he can compete with some of the top players in the country.

in the country in April 1999. He had scored his long-awaited first goal in Cheltenham colours in a 2-1 home win over Doncaster Rovers on 24 October 1998.

He missed the start of Cheltenham's Football League adventure through an injury sustained in the Robins' last match as a non-League club – a 3-0 County Cup victory over Gloucester City. Duff returned to action and took the step up in his stride after making his League debut against Rotherham United on 2 October 1999. He operated as a full-back in the non-League days, but he was asked to play centre half against Rotherham – a position Cotterill always knew he would grow into. Despite that, he was deployed as a right midfielder for the rest of

Above: Michael Duff in aerial action in the League Two clash with Brighton & Hove Albion on 23 October 1999, which finished goalless.

Right: Duff clears his lines for Cheltenham against Kidderminster in an Aggborough draw.

Jason Eaton
Striker, 1992-1999

The name Jason Eaton is permanently etched in Robins' folklore after the prolific marksman scored Cheltenham's winning goal in the 1998 FA Trophy final at Wembley. Eaton played a major part in the Robins' rise and his 115 goals in 248 starts for the club make him the third highest scorer of all time behind Dave Lewis and Jimmy Smith.

He joined Cheltenham in 1992 for £15,000, making the move up the A40 from Gloucester. He had started his career at Bristol City and also played for Bristol Rovers, making him one of the few players to represent both Bristol clubs. During his spell at Rovers, he played under Bobby Gould, who was boss between 1985 and 1987 and was later to manage Cheltenham in 2003. He left Rovers and turned out for non-League clubs Clevedon Town and Trowbridge Town before joining City in 1990. He scored his first goal against Notts County, but

when manager Joe Jordan was replaced by Jimmy Lumsden, Eaton was told that he didn't feature in the new boss' plans.

After joining Cheltenham, Eaton soon struck up a lethal partnership with Smith and the pair scored freely throughout the Robins' five-year spell in the Southern League between 1992 and 1997. He particularly enjoyed the 1995/96 campaign as he scored over 20 goals and was named as Supporters', Players' and Manager's Player of the Year. He always seemed to raise his game for local derbies against Gloucester and could always expect a verbal tirade from the Tigers' fans. He scored in a 5-1 win in 1992/93 and also in a 2-1 victory on Boxing Day 1995. He then scored two against City in a 3-0 triumph at Easter in 1996. Eaton's header also knocked City out of the 1995/96 Dr Marten's Cup, sealing a 1-0 win.

Eaton had more than his fair share of injuries in his early years at Whaddon Road, but he was a vital component in Cheltenham's promotion to the Conference, where he came into his own. He formed another deadly partnership in attack for the Robins, this time with new signing Dale Watkins, also from Gloucester. The pair netted over 50 goals between them during the 1997/98 season and were one of the main factors in Cheltenham's Trophy glory and runners-up finish in the League. Watkins' pace and Eaton's ability to hold the ball up with his back to goal meant that the two worked extremely well together.

After taking the step up in his stride, Eaton scored three goals in Cheltenham's first four Conference matches. He scored their first goal back at the higher level in a 2-1 win against Hayes and hit a brace in a 3-2 win over Northwich Victoria. He found himself neck and neck with Halifax's Geoff Horsfield for the title of the league's top scorer for much of the season. When the two came up against each other at Whaddon Road, it was Eaton who emerged on top. Halifax went into the game on 1 November 1997 unbeaten and were running away at the top of the table, but they were soundly beaten 4-0 by a buoyant Cheltenham side and Eaton helped himself to a hat-trick. Bob Bloomer was the Robins' other goalscorer that day.

The Robins found themselves a goal down in the first leg of the Trophy semi-final against Dover at Whaddon Road. Steve Cotterill threw Eaton on and the goal-poacher turned the tie on its head, scoring two late goals to give Cheltenham the advantage. He then scored in the second leg, which was his 100th goal for the club, as the game finished 2-2 and Cheltenham

49

Jason Eaton during the 1995/96 campaign which saw him win all the club's Player of the Year awards.

made it to the twin towers. After helping Cheltenham to their highest ever finish, Eaton made the trip to the Trophy final and had to postpone his stag night, which was due to take place the same weekend in Liverpool. In the seventy-ninth minute, he headed home Russell Milton's free-kick after a Jamie Victory flick-on, sending the 18,000 fans who had made the trip from Gloucestershire wild. The Cheltenham team for the FA Trophy final was: S. Book; M. Duff, C. Banks, M. Freeman, J. Victory; K. Knight (J. Smith), B. Bloomer, L. Howells, C. Walker (R. Milton); J. Eaton, D. Watkins. Sub not used: D. Wright.

Eaton finished the 1997/98 season with 22 goals and the following year he was part of the Cheltenham squad that won the Conference in only their second season back in the top flight of non-League football. He then made the difficult decision to leave the club as he did not want

to give up his job in the fitness industry as the Robins turned professional.

Cotterill once described Eaton, or 'Bobble' as he was sometimes called by his old boss, as the sort of person he wouldn't mind one of his daughters marrying. Eaton returned to play for Cheltenham's reserve team to regain match fitness during the club's first season in the Football League and demonstrated his knack of scoring with a poacher's goal at Aggborough against Kidderminster's second team. Since leaving Cheltenham, Eaton has played for Yeovil Town, Newport County, Forest Green Rovers, Merthyr Tydfil (two spells), Basingstoke, Bath City, where he was reunited with another Cheltenham favourite Russell Milton, Brislington, Mangotsfield United with old pal Lee Howells, who is now manager of the Bristol club, and Clevedon Town.

Current club captain John Finnigan is the only player to have appeared for Cheltenham Town in both of their play-off final triumphs. Wakefield-born Finnigan was signed by Steve Cotterill from Lincoln City, where he was skipper, in March 2002 as cover for Lee Howells, who broke his leg in a League Two match against Bristol Rovers. Cotterill captured the signature of Finnigan from cash-strapped Lincoln just two days after Howells' injury and the twenty-six-year-old made his debut against York City and scored in an emphatic 4-0 victory for the Robins. He had only scored 3 goals in 143 League appearances for Lincoln, but his fine debut strike suggested that he had the potential to be rather more prolific at Cheltenham. One of his rare Lincoln goals came against the Robins in January 2000 in a 2-0 win at Whaddon Road.

Finnigan's second appearance for Cheltenham was against his former club and he was given a rousing reception by the Imps' fans before the match. Cheltenham won 1-0 at Sincil Bank, with Julian Alsop scoring the winner, and Finnigan had settled quickly into the Robins' midfield alongside Mark Yates. He had already played in Division Two for Lincoln and appeared at Whaddon Road in an FA Cup first round tie which second division Lincoln won 1-0 against Conference side Cheltenham during the 1998/99 season. Lincoln were relegated at the end of that season, while Cheltenham were promoted, so Finnigan's initial aim after signing for Cheltenham was to help his new club into the third tier of English football for the first time.

He had started out as a schoolboy and a trainee at Nottingham Forest, where he played under Brian Clough, Stuart Pearce, Frank Clark and Dave Bassett, who sold him to Lincoln on deadline day 1998 and he helped the club conclude their promotion to Division Two that season. He matched that achievement during his first three months at Cheltenham,

appearing in the play-off semi-final against Hartlepool United after they had missed out on automatic promotion on the final day of the regular season at Plymouth Argyle. A late Neil Grayson goal earned Cheltenham a 1-1 draw at Victoria Park and the second leg also ended all-square resulting in a nerve-wracking penalty shoot-out. Finnigan stepped up to slot home Cheltenham's fourth penalty calmly and Julian Alsop converted their fifth. Richie Humphreys missed for Hartlepool and Cheltenham were in the Millennium Stadium final, where they would face old rivals Rushden and Diamonds. He started the final in the centre of midfield with Yates as Cheltenham produced an excellent performance to claim a deserved 3-1 triumph. Finnigan scored the third goal after eighty minutes to put the match beyond Rushden's reach. The Cheltenham team that day was: S. Book; A. Griffin, M. Duff, R. Walker, J. Victory; L. Williams, M. Yates, J. Finnigan, M. Devaney (N. Grayson); T. Naylor, J. Alsop. Subs not used: M. Lee, N. Tyson, C. Muggleton, N. Howarth.

Finnigan made 12 League appearances, 3 play-off appearances and scored 3 goals during the 2001/02 season. Cotterill departed for Stoke City and Graham Allner first handed Finnigan, who signed a two-year contract, the captaincy at Cheltenham and nicknamed the hardworking midfielder 'the wasp'. Finnigan played in 34 of Cheltenham's 46 matches in the old Division Two, scoring once against Cardiff City under the caretaker managership of Chris Banks, Mark Yates and Bob Bloomer after Allner's sacking in January 2003. He played against Norwich City at Carrow Road in the League Cup where Cheltenham stunned the Division One side with a 3-0 win.

But Cheltenham slipped back to the basement division after just one season and Finnigan made thirty-two appearances the following year as they finished fourteenth and John Ward took over as manager from Bobby Gould, who resigned on 18 October 2003. Finnigan scored one League goal against his former club Lincoln City in a thrilling 3-2 win at Whaddon Road and was appointed club captain following Mark Yates' departure.

Opposite and above: Finnigan in action.

Right: John Finnegan celebrates Cheltenham's League Two play-off triumph at Cardiff's Millennium Stadium in May 2006.

Another thirty-one appearances followed during the 2004/05 season as Cheltenham finished fourteenth again and he found the net in League matches against Mansfield in a 2-1 away win and scored his first brace against Leyton Orient in a 3-2 victory at Brisbane Road. He also scored against Dagenham and Redbridge in a 5-1 LDV Vans first round win.

Undoubtedly his best season yet in Cheltenham colours arrived in 2005/06 as he led Ward's young team to promotion via the play-offs. Finnigan made 48 starts with another 4 substitute appearances and surpassed his best goals tally for one season with 6. His finest performance came against Newcastle United in the FA Cup fourth round tie as the Premiership club were made to work hard for their 2-0 win at Whaddon Road. His most important goal came in the play-off semi-final first leg against Wycombe Wanderers and gave Cheltenham a 1-0 lead. The Robins went on to win 2-1 and draw 0-0 in the second leg to book their second trip to the final. Finnigan led the team out at Cardiff and was his usual energetic self in the centre of midfield, with Grant McCann, as Cheltenham won 1-0 thanks to Steve Guinan's second half strike. He agreed a new two-year contract as he turned thirty and was one of the team's star performers as he won promotion to League One for the third time in his career. At the start of the 2006/07 season he had made 170 starts for Cheltenham and scored 15 goals.

Mark Freeman
Defender, 1996-2001

When Mark Freeman signed for Cheltenham in February 1996, he had already been deemed not good enough to make it as a professional at Wolves and unfit to play in the Conference for Hednesford Town. By the time the big defender had moved on to Boston United in 2001 after a glorious spell at Whaddon Road, he had proved a lot of people wrong.

'Boka', as he was universally known thanks to his grandmother (his brothers were known as 'Doopy' and 'Bloggsy'!), started his career at Southern League Midland Division Bilston Town as a sixteen-year-old. He spent two years at Wolves – the club he supported as a boy – and was in the Wanderers' squad when they beat Cheltenham 5-1 at Molineux in the FA Cup first round in 1987, with Steve Bull netting his first Wolves hat-trick. He returned to non-League football with Willenhall Town after leaving Wolves in 1989 without appearing for the first team. Hednesford paid £5,000 for his services and he formed a successful central defensive partnership with Steve Essex for the Pitmen as they stormed to the Southern League title in 1995, with Cheltenham having to settle for the runners-up spot. After a brief spell at Gloucester City following his release from Conference-bound Hednesford, Cheltenham boss Chris Robinson paid £7,500 to bring Freeman up the Golden Valley. He once described his move to Gloucester as the biggest mistake of his career and he made his Robins debut in a 1-1 draw at Baldock Town on 24 February 1996.

He soon helped to shore up a leaky Cheltenham defence that had struggled after Steve Jones' departure to Swansea earlier in the season. Freeman notched his first Robins goal against Burton Albion in a 1-0 home win and he forged an immediate understanding with Chris Banks. The duo went on to form arguably the most formidable defensive pairing in Cheltenham's history, playing together for the next five and a half seasons. At 6ft 2ins and in excess of fourteen stone, Freeman was never blessed with much pace, but with his dominating physical approach and Banks' football brain and reading of the game, the two were an ideal combination.

Freeman's first full season saw the Robins claim promotion to the Conference under Steve Cotterill and he soon proved he was highly capable of playing at the higher standard despite what Hednesford boss John Baldwin had thought two years earlier. Baldwin later admitted that letting Freeman go was his biggest mistake. Walsall-born Freeman was left out of the opening Conference game at Dover which the Robins lost 3-0, but he was swiftly recalled and excelled against the leading strikers outside the Football League. He played a vital role in Cheltenham's FA Trophy success at Wembley in 1998, making 43 appearances and scoring 2 goals during the 1997/98 campaign. He was also a huge influence as Cotterill's men claimed the Conference Championship the following year, making 47 appearances and scoring 6 goals.

Above: Mark Freeman enjoys himself during Chris Banks' benefit match against Aston Villa in 2000.

Left: Freeman challenges Southend goalkeeper Mel Capleton in a 2-1 defeat for Cheltenham at Roots Hall in May 2000.

Freeman, with his imposing physique and uncompromising style, was a key figure for the Robins between 1996 and 2001.

He headed home the crucial equalising goal at Rushden & Diamonds on 3 April 1999 on the day the title race changed direction in a matter of seconds. Neil Grayson scored the winner to earn Cheltenham an improbable 2-1 win. It was especially sweet for Freeman, who had been controversially sent off at Nene Park during his previous visit when Cheltenham were beaten 4-1 in 1998. Freeman was described by Cotterill as the 'Colossus' of his defence as Cheltenham entered the world of professional football for the first time, and he made his Football League debut at the age of twenty-nine against Rochdale on 7 August 1999. He gave up his day job as a window maker and scored his first Division Three goal against Carlisle United in a 3-1 win. His defensive partnership with Banks continued to flourish as Cheltenham made a late charge towards the play-offs.

The Robins narrowly missed out on the play-offs in each of their first two seasons in the League and the 2000/01 season was a frustrating one for Freeman. He struggled with back problems that kept him sidelined for much of the second half of the campaign. He joined Conference club Boston United in the summer of 2001 for £15,000 after 224 starting appearances and 6 as a substitute. He also scored a total of 16 goals for the Robins. His final appearance was from the bench in a 1-0 home win over Exeter City on 3 March 2001.

Freeman was a big man with a big heart; he played a key role in Cheltenham's rise through the leagues and helped them to become established as a professional club. He was in the crowd for Cheltenham's FA Cup fifth round tie at West Bromwich Albion in 2002 and was given a great reception by the Robins' fans who held him in such high esteem throughout his time at Whaddon Road.

Joe Gadston
Striker, 1966-1968, 1973

Much-travelled striker Joe Gadston was voted Cheltenham Town's Player of the Year in 1967/68. A former West Ham United amateur, he turned professional for Brentford in August 1964, but failed to secure a first team slot at Griffin Park and joined non-League outfit Corby Town in July 1966. He moved to Cheltenham five months later and made his debut in a 2-1 home win over Burton Albion on 19 November 1966. He scored his first Robins goal a week later against Guildford City in another 2-1 success.

He scored 13 goals from 33 appearances in his first half season in the red and white of Cheltenham, including a hat-trick against Bath City in April 1967 and he quickly became a huge hit with the Whaddon Road faithful. He also scored a brace against Bedford Town on New Year's Eve in a 3-1 win as Cheltenham finished thirteenth in the Southern League Premier Division.

He shrugged off an early season injury and was leading marksman during the 1967/68 campaign scoring 26 goals in 51 games. The successful season saw Cheltenham finish fourth in the Southern League and Gadston was named as the club's best player by the fans. Gadston scored another treble against Cambridge City and bagged braces against Wimbledon and Barry Town, but the highlight of his time at Cheltenham came against Barnet, when he scored all four goals in a 4-0 success over the Bees on 26 February 1968.

His final Cheltenham appearance came against Chelmsford City on the last day of the season in a 1-1 draw at Whaddon Road and his final goal had arrived ten days earlier in a 3-1 win at Hastings United, where Willie Ferns scored twice. After 39 goals in 84 appearances for Cheltenham, Gadston was sold to Bristol Rovers for £1,500 in June 1968. Despite scoring twice for Rovers on his home debut against AFC Bournemouth, he was unable to hold down a regular place in their third division side and joined Exeter City for £1,500 in November 1969.

The skilful Gadston partnered ace hitman Alan Banks in the Grecians' attack and moved to Aldershot on a free transfer in July 1972. He briefly rejoined Cheltenham on loan in January 1973. He was also loaned to Hartlepool before joining Wimbledon in July 1973. Moving to Hillingdon Borough in March 1974, Gadston then had spells with Walton and Hersham, Slough Town, Hayes, Ruislip Manor and Hanwell Town as player-manager.

He subsequently became Brentford's youth development officer under Steve Perryman, who was in charge at Griffin Park from 1987 to 1990. He then ran a holiday business in Swanage and became general manager of Swanage Town and Herston FC in July 1996. He also had a brief spell as a director at Exeter City with whom he visited Whaddon Road during the Robins' Football League clash with the Devon club in 1999/00.

Peter Goring
Striker, 1945-1947

He spent the first eighteen months of his time at Arsenal playing for the reserves, but went on to skipper the Gunners and play in the 1950 FA Cup final at Wembley Stadium in front of more than 100,000 fans. Arsenal beat Liverpool 2-0 that day with Goring starting the game up front as Reg Lewis scored both of the Gunners' goals. Several coach loads of Cheltenham followers made their way to Wembley to cheer Goring on in the final.

Goring scored 16 goals the following season for Arsenal, but was displaced by Cliff Holton in 1951/52 and suffered a drop in form, only managing five goals during the campaign. He fought his way back into the side during the 1952/53 season and rediscovered his goalscoring touch, notching 10 goals in 29 appearances as Arsenal claimed the old First Division title for the seventh time in their history. The goals dried up again for Goring in the 1953/54 season and he was switched to right half by Arsenal boss Tom Whittaker, who was at the Highbury helm from 1947 to 1956. He adapted well to his new role and reclaimed a regular place in the starting line-up.

Peter Goring joined then-Southern League outfit Cheltenham as a raw youngster in 1945, signed by then-manager Jimmy Brain who was in charge at Whaddon Road from 1937 to 1948. Cheltenham used 51 players in just 32 games during the 1945/46 season, and Goring was vital at centre forward, scoring 25 goals. Goring's first goals for the club came when he struck twice in a 2-2 draw at Barry Town. He played for the Robins against Aldershot in the FA Cup first round proper and fired four goals in a match against Yeovil Town. Goring had impressed Arsenal in a friendly match the previous season and he had already scored 62 goals in 90 outings for the Robins when Arsenal made their move for him. He became Cheltenham's most expensive transfer when he joined Arsenal for £1,500 midway through the 1947/48 season. He signed off with a goal for Cheltenham in a 1-1 Southern League Cup draw with Chelmsford City.

Goring scored 53 goals from 240 appearances in his ten years at Highbury and after leaving Arsenal in the summer of 1959, he played for non-League club Romford, before managing Cheltenham's reserve team and later Forest Green Rovers. One of his players at Forest Green was John Murphy, who went on to manage Cheltenham Town from 1983 to 1988, and again in 1990.

Goring passed away at the age of sixty-seven in 1994. He was held in very high esteem at Highbury and eight former players – Peter Goy, Ray Daniels, Joe Wade, Arthur Milton, Derek Tapscott, Dave Bowen, Ben Marsden and Cliff Holton – travelled to his funeral at St Michael's and All Angels' Church in Bishop's Cleeve to pay their respects to one of the finest footballers to hail from Gloucestershire.

Bill Gourlay was not a particularly big goalkeeper, standing at only 5ft 10ins and weighing 12st 3lbs in his early twenties, but what he lacked in size he made up for in athleticism, speed and bravery. He was born in Stoneyburn, West Lothian and began his career across the River Forth with Cowdenbeath in the Scottish League. He made a big enough impression with Cowdenbeath to be sold for a record fee to Manchester City, who made Gourlay understudy to their legendary goalkeeper, Bert Trautmann. After two seasons with City and no sign of a first team place, Gourlay was placed on the transfer list at his own request and Anderson, through his contacts in Scotland, arranged for him to join Cheltenham Town in the summer of 1954.

He made his debut on the opening day of the season, a 4-2 defeat at Gravesend & Northfleet in the Southern League but went on to miss only one match in the remainder of the season as Cheltenham finished fourth in the division. Over the next five seasons the Robins were never out of the top six in a strong Southern League. He played in the team that finished runners-up to Guildford City in 1955/56, keeping fourteen clean sheets along the way and putting in a brilliant display as the Robins won 1-0 at Chelmsford City (one of the strongest clubs outside the Football League back then) despite losing centre half Joe Hyde to an injury early in the game. Gourlay also played in the cup run of 1956/57 that ended with a record attendance at Whaddon Road of 8,326 for the visit of Reading in the first round. He was in goal for all the matches, including both legs of the final, as Cheltenham Town won the Southern League Cup for the first and only time in 1957/58. He also kept a clean sheet against Watford in the FA Cup in 1959/60 as the Hornets were held to a 0-0 draw at Whaddon Road, before winning the replay 3-0.

Gourlay was awarded a benefit game along with Augie Scott and Sid Dunn against Wycombe Wanderers in November 1959 and the players also received a share of the gate receipts from that year's county cup tie at home to Gloucester City in recognition of their service to the club.

Widely regarded as one of the club's greatest ever goalkeepers, Gourlay was at Cheltenham Town for a total of eight seasons and missed only a handful of matches until injury disrupted the 1961/62 campaign. His absence was a factor, along with disruptions both on and off the pitch, in Cheltenham Town suffering their first ever relegation during 1961/62. He made a total of 379 first-team appearances in all competitions for Cheltenham Town and left in 1962 to remain in the Southern League Premier Division with Weymouth.

Andy Gray
Striker, 1989-1990

The 1989/90 season will always be remembered as the year that Andy Gray came to play for Cheltenham Town. Gray only played 29 matches for the Robins and scored 6 goals, but he took Cheltenham into the national spotlight and became one of the most famous players ever to represent the club. The signing of the former Scottish international was a major coup for manager Jim Barron on 14 August 1989. Gray made his debut in a 1-1 draw with Hinckley Town in the Midland Floodlit Cup, but it took him twelve matches to net his first goal against Chorley on 21 October in a 2-0 win. His arrival at Whaddon Road caused great excitement and the average crowd increased from 1,295 the previous year to 1,423 and the fourteen per cent rise was in no small part due to Gray's presence at the club.

Gray was a household name after a professional career that saw him win virtually every major honour in the English game. Born in Drumchapel, Glasgow on 30 November 1955,

Gray started his career at Dundee United in 1973 and made his name as an effective striker. He moved south of the border and signed for Aston Villa and he was named as both PFA Player and Young Player of the Year in 1977 before joining Wolverhampton Wanderers in a then-club record £1.5 million deal in 1979. After scoring the winning goal for Wolves in the 1980 League Cup final against Nottingham Forest, he moved to Everton in 1983 for £250,000.

He appeared in the FA Cup final for Everton as the Toffees defeated Watford 2-0, scoring the second goal after fifty-one minutes following Graeme Sharp's opener to earn Everton their first FA Cup win since 1966. The next season was the most successful in Everton's proud history as they won the Charity Shield, the League Championship and the European Cup-Winners' Cup. They beat Bayern Munich in the semi-finals of the Cup-Winners' Cup with Gray scoring one and making two in the 3-1 second leg win following a goalless first leg in Germany. Howard Kendall's Merseysiders beat Rapid Vienna 3-1 in the final in Rotterdam, with Gray, Kevin Sheedy and Trevor Steven scoring the goals to earn the club their only European trophy to date on 15 May 1985. They were denied a treble by Manchester United, who beat them 1-0 after extra time in the FA Cup final at Wembley.

Gray, who won 20 caps for Scotland, moved back to his native land to join childhood heroes Glasgow Rangers after his successful stint at Goodison Park. He helped Rangers to the first of their nine successive League championships in 1988/89 before joining Cheltenham in a shock move. He produced a number of committed performances for the Robins, scoring against Enfield at Southbury Road, twice at Chorley, once in a 4-0 home win over Farnborough Town and in a 5-1 FA Trophy first round win over Gravesend and Northfleet after his first Conference goal against Chorley at Whaddon Road. Cheltenham bowed out of the Trophy to Kingstonian in the third round after a replay and the 3-0 humbling on 28 February

Andy Gray of Sky Sports fame playing for Cheltenham during the 1989/90 Conference campaign.

1990 proved to be Gray's last outing in the red and white of Cheltenham.

He went on to play a central role in the development of football coverage for the satellite channel Sky Sports, earning a variety of accolades including the Royal Television Society's Sports Presenter of the Year. He remains a hugely popular and respected commentator and his autobiography *Gray Matters* was published in 2004.

Neil Grayson

Striker, 1998-2002

FA Trophy, their first major piece of silverware. Grayson was to contribute as much as anyone to Cheltenham's second – the Conference Championship – twelve months later.

Grayson had already played at Wembley, for Northampton Town in a Division Three play-off final victory over Swansea. His career started in the more modest surroundings of Rowntree Mackintosh. He made the step up to full-time football at a relatively late age, joining Doncaster Rovers at the age of twenty-five. He scored 6 goals in 29 League appearances in his two seasons at Belle Vue. He then made one appearance for his home town team York City, before joining Chesterfield. Grayson dropped out of the League in 1992 and played for Gateshead and Boston United in the Conference. He moved back to the pro game in 1994 when he joined Northampton. He spent three successful seasons with the Cobblers, making 120 League appearances and hitting 31 goals. Following Hereford's relegation to the Conference in 1997, Bulls boss Graham Turner paid £25,000 to Northampton for the services of Grayson, hoping that his goals would fire Hereford back into the League. However, Turner was soon forced to let his star players leave Edgar Street and Steve Cotterill took full advantage.

One of the first opportunities for Cheltenham fans to see Grayson in action came in an England semi-professional international, against the Netherlands at Crawley's Broadfield Stadium. Grayson had just signed for Cheltenham and he partnered fellow Robin Dale Watkins in attack for England. Grayson scored on his international debut as John Owens' side won 2-1. Grayson's debut for Cheltenham was a day to forget for the Robins as they were reduced to nine men and beaten 4-1 at Rushden's Nene Park. It took time for Grayson to win over the Whaddon Road faithful, but it was not long before he began to show what he was capable of. He hit 6 goals in 13 starts in the 1997/98 season including a brace at Farnborough in a 2-1 win.

There were many eyebrows raised around Whaddon Road when Steve Cotterill splashed out £18,000 on a thirty-three-year-old forward in 1998. Some thought that Hereford United's Neil Grayson was past his best, but they could not have been more wrong. In reality, he turned out to be arguably Steve Cotterill's best signing and financially stricken Hereford's loss was very much Cheltenham's gain. Grayson had tormented Cheltenham at Edgar Street early on in their first year back in the Conference. He scored two, including a thirty-yard screamer, past Steve Book in the Bulls' 3-2 victory in August 1997. By the end of the season he was helping Cheltenham claim the runners–up spot behind runaway leaders Halifax Town.

Grayson was the first of the 'famous four' who Cheltenham recruited from Hereford and was signed by Cotterill with the following season's assault on the title firmly in mind. He was cup-tied and therefore forced to watch from the stands as Cheltenham beat Southport to lift the

After a slow start to the 1998/99 season, Cheltenham climbed to the top of the Conference table and Grayson began to start

scoring some special goals. His solo effort against Morecambe in a 4-1 home win was one of the goals of the season and epitomised the determination that was a key feature of his game. Grayson scored the equaliser in a 1-1 home draw with Woking that sent the Robins flying to the top of the table for the first time in their history. He also produced a wonderful individual display in the 3-0 win over title rivals Kettering that put Cheltenham in the driving seat at the top of the table.

The date of 3 April 1999 is one that no Cheltenham fan will forget and Grayson scored one of his most important goals for the club. Trailing 1-0 at Rushden's Nene Park in the Championship showdown, Cheltenham scored two late goals to snatch a vital win. It was Grayson who scrambled home the winner after

Mark Freeman had headed Cheltenham level. Grayson's goal came as many fans were still celebrating 'Boka's' equaliser and sparked scenes of even wilder celebrations that are unlikely to be equalled. Grayson followed up that priceless winner with two more in quick succession. He scored the only goals in two crucial home wins over Kidderminster and Kingstonian, which put Cheltenham on the brink of the title.

He developed a habit of scoring in the most important games and this continued with goals in both legs of the FA Trophy semi-final against Kingstonian. The K's emerged victorious and it was their turn to visit the twin towers, but Grayson was soon at it again in the League. He scored Cheltenham's second goal in the thrilling 3-2 triumph over Yeovil that clinched promotion to the Football League. At the age

Neil Grayson

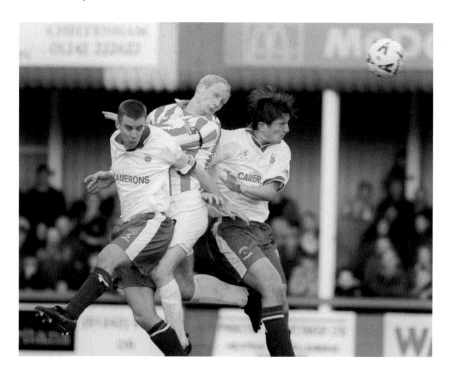

of thirty-four, Grayson would be returning to full-time football. He still had time to be named as Cheltenham's Player of the Year, Conference Player of the Year and to earn more England semi-pro caps to round off a memorable season all round for the Yorkshireman. Grayson also had the Cheltenham Town badge tattooed on his arm as a sign of his devotion to the club.

After scoring so many important goals in Cheltenham's non-League days, it was no surprise when Grayson thundered home an Antony Griffin cross against Mansfield to give the Robins their first Football League goal and subsequently, their first win. Grayson topped the scoring charts with 10 League goals during Cheltenham's Football League bow. He fired home a penalty in the 2-1 second leg win over Norwich City in the League Cup. He also scored against his home town team York in the freezing festive victory, but the pick of Grayson's goals came in a 2-0 home win over Plymouth Argyle. Steve Book's long kick was flicked on to Grayson, who unleashed an incredible forty-yard volley to leave the whole ground

breathless and register one of the great strikes at Whaddon Road. The previous week, Grayson had received a standing ovation as he returned to Northampton Town's Sixfields Stadium. It was clear that the Cobblers' fans held Grayson in very high esteem and many cheered as he scored a trademark near post header against their team. Northampton eventually won 3-2, but it was Grayson's night.

He started the 2000/01 season in familiar fashion, bagging a brace against York at Bootham Crescent, but he paid a price. He broke an ankle scoring his second and faced a lengthy spell on the sidelines. He returned to action and top scored for the club for the third season running. He netted 13 League goals, including a memorable hat-trick against Cardiff. It included one with his right foot, one with his head and then one with his trusty left to earn Cheltenham a fine 3-1 win over the promotion chasing Bluebirds.

During his fifth and final season at Cheltenham, Grayson was a largely peripheral figure, but still played his part in Cheltenham's

Neil Grayson looking for goals in Cheltenham's first ever FA Cup fourth round tie, against Burnley in 2002.

promotion success. He scored in the first league win of the season against Carlisle, but the form of Julian Alsop and Tony Naylor meant that he struggled to make the starting XI. He played an important role in Cheltenham's play-off semi-final win over Hartlepool. The first leg saw Cheltenham trailing as the game reached the closing minutes, but Grayson popped up to score a priceless equaliser. He then put away his spot-kick in the dramatic second leg shoot-out to help seal a place in the final. Grayson came off the bench at the Millennium Stadium and as usual it didn't take him long to make an impact. He crashed a fierce shot against the crossbar and John Finnigan fired home the rebound to give Cheltenham an unassailable 3-1 lead. Grayson was in possession of the ball as the final whistle blew and it was to be his last appearance for the club. He waved a tearful goodbye to the fans during the open-top bus tour of the town as the team paraded their play-off trophy.

Grayson would give anything for the cause and was a defenders' nightmare with his never-say-die attitude. He was always willing to stick his head in where boots were flying and it became almost customary for him to go down injured with a knock to his head, but he always got back up and was soon looking for more. He joined Forest Green Rovers at the age of thirty-eight, top scoring for his new club in the 2002/03 Conference campaign. He then moved to Stafford Rangers and hit two goals on his debut for the Southern League side. He followed that up with two more against Bath City. The forty-one-year-old helped Stafford win promotion to the Conference National at the end of the 2005/06 season. He still has a passion for the game and it will be no surprise if he continues to play long into his forties. Howard Wilkinson once described Grayson as 'the heart of football' and it is an accurate description of a true Cheltenham Town legend.

Forest of Dean-born Gerald Horlick has the honour of having been Cheltenham Town's first ever Player of the Year at the end of the 1965/66 season.

Horlick started out as a junior at Bristol City, where he appeared for the youth team, but he turned down the chance to sign professional forms on his eighteenth birthday when his mother insisted he completed his apprenticeship as a carpenter at C.H. Hunt builders in Drybrook.

He signed for the Robins from Gloucester City in the summer of 1964, joining a Cheltenham team that had just won promotion to the Southern Premier Division. He had been a regular scorer for the Tigers under the management of Ollie Norris, but Cheltenham boss Arch Anderson secured his services and he made his debut in a 2-1 Southern League Cup defeat to Rugby Town. He scored his first goal for the club in the second leg as Rugby were defeated 3-1. He went on to score 13 goals in 28 appearances during his first season. Horlick partnered the likes of Bobby Grant, Joe Gadston and Ralph Norton in attack and his strong, determined style made him a handful for opposition defences.

As well as taking the Player of the Year trophy, he was also Cheltenham's top scorer during the 1965/66 campaign with 23 goals in 42 games. Horlick led the forward line for six seasons and his partnership with Gadston was particularly fruitful during the memorable 1967/68 campaign. The Robins challenged for the Southern League title and eventually finished fourth behind Wimbledon, Chelmsford City and Cambridge United. Horlick also helped the club reach the 1968/69 Southern League Cup final.

After 107 goals in 259 appearances for Cheltenham, Horlick left the club at the end of the 1969/70 season and retired due to a knee injury. His replacement was a young lad signed from local football by the name of Dave Lewis, who of course went on to smash the club's goal-scoring record over the next thirteen years.

Horlick worked for Rank Xerox in Mitcheldean as a maintenance carpenter for thirteen years after leaving the Robins. He then held a similar post at Gloucester Royal Hospital and the Forest Unit until retiring in September 1995. He was one of the former greats to appear on 'Legends Day' at Whaddon Road for the launch of the Robins Trust in the summer of 2005, along with his friend, golfing partner and former Robins teammate Roger Thorndale. Gerald's son Andy played for the Robins' reserve team during the 1991/92 season after starring for the club's successful youth team.

Gerald Horlick leaps highest for Cheltenham Town at Burton Albion's Eton Park.

S teve Cotterill once described Lee Howells as the 'jewel in the crown' of Cheltenham's FA Trophy and Conference winning sides. It was an accurate description of a player who will be remembered as one of the club's true greats. An Australian-born dual-national, 'Archie', as he is universally known, was involved in three promotions, two relegations, glorious cup exploits and served under seven different managers. He is fourth in the all-time list of appearance makers with 450 starts for the club and 77 goals behind only Roger Thorndale, Dave Lewis and Jamie Victory.

It was Ally Robertson who signed Howells in November 1991 on the recommendation of Lindsay Parsons. Parsons knew Howells from his days as a youngster at Bristol Rovers and it was not long before Parsons was installed as boss at Whaddon Road. The club were struggling at the foot of the Conference and Howells was powerless to prevent relegation at the end of his first season. Howells made his debut for Cheltenham at right-back alongside Mark Buckland, Anton Vircavs and Kevin Willetts. Wycombe Wanderers were the opponents and Howells found himself up against a young Steve Guppy. His first Cheltenham goal came in his third appearance at Altrincham in a 2-1 defeat on 14 December 1991. He also scored in the 3-2 win over Welling United on the final day of the season, but it was not enough to save the Robins from the drop and they were relegated by two points in twenty-first place along with basement club Barrow.

Howells soon switched to the centre of midfield and made the number seven shirt his own for over a decade. He made 45 appearances during the 1992/93 season and scored 13 goals when Cheltenham finished as runners-up to Dover Athletic. He scored 12 goals in 50 appearances the following year as Cheltenham missed out on promotion again, this time finishing second behind Farnborough Town. During the 1994/95 season Howells scored in the 8-0 win over Corby Town and hit two late goals to rescue a 2-2 draw at Worcester City at Christmas. He made 42 appearances and scored 14 goals as Cheltenham finished as runners-up for the third year in succession. Howells came very close to signing for Gillingham after Parsons left Cheltenham to become assistant manager to Tony Pulis at the Priestfield Stadium club. The move fell through, but injury restricted him to just 16 appearances during the 1995/96 season as new boss Chris Robinson guided his team to third place behind Rushden and Diamonds and Halesowen Town.

The entire club was transformed during the following campaign after Steve Cotterill took over as manager and Howells began to show some of his best form in a Cheltenham shirt. He was influential in Cheltenham's promotion to the Conference in 1997 and he continued to be at the centre of the club's rapid progress. He received England semi-professional honours during the 1997/98 season and made his

Lee Howells heads clear in a GM Vauxhall Conference clash during the 1991/92 season.

England debut against Holland at Crawley's Broadfield Stadium in a 2-1 win. He starred for Cheltenham as they claimed the Conference runners-up spot behind Halifax Town. They also reached the third round of the FA Cup and beat Southport at Wembley to lift the FA Trophy. The club had become more professional under Cotterill and this brought out the best in Howells, whose ability had never been in doubt. He established himself as one of the leading players in non-League football as Cheltenham went one step better the following season and won the Conference title.

After a much deserved benefit game against Wolves in July 1999, Howells made his Football League debut at the age of thirty. He played in 45 of Cheltenham's 46 League fixtures in their first season in the professional ranks. Howells was pivotal to Cheltenham's 2001/02 promotion bid and he also played a major role in Cheltenham's groundbreaking run to round five of the FA Cup. He played alongside Mark Yates in every round as Cheltenham pulled off shock wins over Oldham and Burnley. They eventually bowed out to West Brom at the Hawthorns in front of over 27,000 fans. Shortly after the West Brom defeat, an in-form Howells was looking forward to playing against the club where his career began – Bristol Rovers – at the Memorial Stadium. In an innocuous challenge with Pirates' midfielder Vitalijs Astafjevs, he suffered a broken tibia and fibula, ruling him out of the play-off final victory at the Millennium Stadium and the whole of the next season. He had done as much as anyone to help Cheltenham into Division Two, but never played at the higher level.

As Cheltenham dropped back to Division Three, Howells was given a great reception as he returned to action in a pre-season friendly against Sheffield United. He made seven starts during the 2003/04 season, including the fine 3-1 FA Cup win over Hull. He was asked to play out of position on the right of midfield and his last appearance was in the defeat at Torquay on 15 November 2003.

After a spell with Merthyr Tydfil, Howells is now the manager of Southern League Premier Division club Mangotsfield United, combining semi-professional football with hairdressing.

helped Cheltenham finish two points ahead of runners-up King's Lynn at the top of the Premier Division table.

Hughes made more appearances than any other Cheltenham player during the club's first season in the Conference, turning out in all 56 of the Robins' matches during the 1985/86 campaign. He scored a brace in the Southern League Challenge match against League Cup winners Fisher Athletic as Cheltenham won 3-2 and he added 10 goals to his total that season. He also found the net in the Robins' first Conference match against Maidstone, with Steve Brooks also on target in a 2-1 win at Whaddon Road in front of 1,082 fans.

Cheltenham played 169 games in Hughes' first three seasons at the club and he appeared in 168 of them. He missed a Conference match against Northwich Victoria on 13 December 1987, which Cheltenham lost 1-0. He played in the other 53 games that season and missed only three matches during the 1987/88 campaign. He had missed only four of the 230 matches Cheltenham had played since he joined the club. He scored a total of 56 goals in 226 starts for Cheltenham and featured in the FA Cup first round trip to Wolverhampton Wanderers during the 1987/88 season. The Robins took a shock lead at Molineux through Brett Angell, but were eventually beaten 5-1. Towards the end of his spell at Whaddon Road, Hughes demonstrated his versatility by often filling in at full-back.

After four highly successful years at Cheltenham, Hughes moved to local rivals Gloucester City in August 1988 for £4,000. He captained the Tigers to the Southern League Midland Division title in 1989 and runners-up spot in the Premier Division in 1991, when Gloucester came agonisingly close to joining Cheltenham in the Conference. After 243 starts and 18 goals for the Tigers and a spell as player-coach under the managerial reign of John Murphy, Hughes left Gloucester with Murphy to join Witney Town in 1996.

He returned to Meadow Park as assistant to Leroy Rosenior, before taking over as boss in

Having started his career at Swindon Town as an apprentice, Brian Hughes made his Football League debut for the Wiltshire club in 1980 away to Reading. He moved to Torquay United in August 1983 and made 42 starts for the Gulls before signing for Cheltenham Town on a free transfer in July 1984. The skilful and highly influential right midfielder was ever-present during his first campaign at Whaddon Road, as Cheltenham won the Southern League title for the first time in their history to clinch promotion to the Gola League (now Conference). Hughes made his debut against Gravesend and Northfleet in a 1-1 draw on 18 August 1984. He scored his first goal against Hastings United a week later in a 1-0 victory. He went on to make 59 appearances and was named as Player of the Year at the end of the memorable season and was also the Robins' second top scorer with 27 goals, an impressive tally from any midfield player. Hughes' consistency and goals

November 1998. He was surprisingly sacked in February 2000 and took over as boss back at Witney in the Southern League Eastern Division. He then joined his old Robins teammate Steve Abbley at Cirencester Town, where he was manager until the end of the 2005/06 season, when he handed in his resignation. He had lifted Cirencester into the Southern League Premier Division for the first time in their history at the end of the 2003/04 season as the Centurions finished third in the Western Division. They finished in a respectable seventh place at the higher level a year later, but they struggled the following season and finally finished eighteenth, narrowly avoiding relegation. This prompted Hughes to step aside and give someone else a chance to take the club forward, but he made an indelible contribution to Cirencester Town and helped oversee the move to their modern Corinium Stadium and impressive Arena facility.

Joe Hyde signed for Cheltenham Town as a sixteen-year-old in 1951 and made his debut as a left-half in a 1-0 win over Yeovil Town on 23 February 1952, but it was while operating at the centre of defence that Hyde became a Robins great. He had been playing for the Colts team in August 1951 and then progressed to the reserve team after being spotted playing for Baker Street in the Youth Division of the Cheltenham League. William Raeside took the managerial reins from George Summerbee in March 1952 and Hyde made nine starts during his first season as Cheltenham finished eighteenth in the Southern League.

He established himself as a first team regular during the 1952/53 campaign, making 38 appearances as Cheltenham finished five places higher than they had twelve months earlier. Hyde became the cornerstone of the Cheltenham backline for a further eight seasons. Hyde was not the tallest of defenders, but what he lacked in height he made up for in strength and athleticism.

He helped Cheltenham to the highest finish in the club's history at the end of the 1955/56 season, making fifty appearances as they finished second behind Guildford City in the Southern League table, four points adrift of the champions, under Scottish manager Arch Anderson. He was prominent in the Robins' FA Cup run during the 1956/57 season as Anderson's men progressed from the preliminary round to the first round proper with victories over Lovells Athletic, Ebbw Vale, Gloucester City, Llanelli and Andover. They were defeated 2-1 in the first round by Reading. Hyde also appeared in the 1957/58 Southern League Cup final as Cheltenham took the silverware knocking out Bath City, Hereford United and Guildford City on their way to a 2-1 final win over Gravesend. He was ever-present that season and he rarely missed a game throughout the rest of his time as a Robin.

Hyde played his final match for the club in a 2-2 draw at Chelmsford City in March 1961 – after appearing in all 43 of the club's League and cup matches up to that point in the 1960/61 season – that saw them finish seventeenth in the Southern League Premier Division.

Hyde made the number five shirt his own and turned out for the Robins more than 400 times between 1952 and 1961. He played in the same Robins team as highly rated goalkeeper Bill Gourlay and record appearance maker Roger Thorndale. After leaving Cheltenham, Hyde played for Gloucester City for three seasons. He moved on to Evesham United before entering management with Cinderford Town.

Popular defender Alan Jefferies is one of a select group of players to have made over 400 appearances for Cheltenham Town. Only Roger Thorndale, Dave Lewis, Joe Hyde, Lee Howells and Jamie Victory have played more games for the Robins. Jefferies was a commanding centre half who joined Cheltenham in the summer of 1967 following his release from Brentford and a brief spell with Banbury United. He made his Robins debut at the start of the 1967/68 season against Margate Athletic in a 3-0 victory on 23 August. He stayed at Whaddon Road for eight seasons and was named as Player of the Year at the end of the 1970/71 campaign.

The son of former Brentford goalkeeper Alf Jefferies, Alan began his playing career under his father's management at Hellenic League club Didcot Town. He appeared briefly for Oxford United's reserve team before joining the Bees in July 1965, but he struggled to break into the first team at Griffin Park due to the form of long-serving Peter Gelson.

Jefferies featured prominently in Bob Etheridge's Cheltenham team that finished fourth in a very strong Southern League in 1968. He was ever-present for two consecutive seasons including the 1968/69 season when the Robins reached the Southern League Cup final. He played in both legs of the final against Cambridge United. Cheltenham lost the away leg 1-0 and a goalless draw at Whaddon Road in the second leg was not enough to win them the cup. Jefferies made a total of 71 appearances that season, including 13 in the Midland Floodlit Cup.

Jefferies was joined at Whaddon Road by his goalkeeping brother Malcolm, who made thirty-three appearances for Cheltenham between 1970 and 1972. Alan starred in three unsuccessful promotion challenges from 1972 to 1974 when the Robins finished third place in First Division (North). He made a total of 403 appearances for Cheltenham, scoring 19 goals, including 13 goals in 291 Southern League outings. He made his 400th appearance against Redditch United in a 2-1 defeat on 10 April 1975, with Dave Lewis scoring Cheltenham's goal. He appeared against Bury Town twice and Worcester City, and the 3-1 defeat to Worcester proved to be his 403rd and final Robins appearance.

He left to join Witney Town in 1975 and helped the Oxfordshire club to the Southern League First Division (North) title in 1977/78. He then moved on to the player-coach's role at Oxford City prior to joining Aylesbury United, featuring in the Ducks' 1981 run to the FA Trophy quarter-finals. He went on to play for Thame United and ran two pubs in the area before moving into sport and leisure management, taking control of the Blackbird Leys Leisure Centre in Oxford.

Nick Jordan

Midfield, 1983-1992

Kings' Lynn. Jordan played 52 times during the triumphant campaign and contributed an important 15 goals as Cheltenham won promotion to the Conference for the first time in their history. One of his most important strikes was a spectacular winner against RS Southampton in an epic 3-2 victory on 24 April 1985 in front of 813 fans at Whaddon Road. The title was secured at the same ground on 4 May as Cheltenham beat Alvechurch 2-1 before 1,999 supporters. Cheltenham missed out on the double after they were beaten over two legs by Fisher Athletic in the League Cup final after beating VS Rugby, Forest Green Rovers, Moor Green and Redditch United en route to the final.

The Robins made the step up to the Conference and Jordan made 29 starts and scored 3 goals in his first season at the higher level. Cheltenham finished a creditable eleventh at the end of their debut season in what was then called the Gola League and Jordan scored against Minehead in the FA Cup first qualifying round defeat, Fisher Athletic in the FA Trophy first round and at home to Dagenham in a 2-2 League draw. Cheltenham repeated their eleventh placed finish in their second season in the Conference and Jordan played 42 matches and scored 5 goals. He scored 7 goals in 37 appearances and the Robins finished thirteenth at the end of the 1987/88 season.

Manager John Murphy resigned after a 3-0 FA Cup second qualifying round defeat at the hands of Gloucester City on 1 October 1988. Jim Barron was appointed as manager and Jordan played 47 games and found the net 7 times as Cheltenham ended the 1988/89 season in sixteenth place. His consistent run continued with 40 appearances and 9 goals during the 1989/90 campaign as Cheltenham equalled their best Conference finish of eleventh. Jordan was rewarded for his sterling service with a joint testimonial with Ray Baverstock in 1990 against a strong Everton team. Neville Southall appeared in goal for Cheltenham and the Robins won the match 1-0.

Jordan had played over 300 matches and scored 60 goals when the ill-fated 1991/92

Nick Jordan arrived at Whaddon Road from his local club Moreton Town in the summer of 1983 to join boss Alan Wood in the club's first season back in the Premier Division of the Southern League. He joined Cheltenham Town as a left-sided forward, but went on to play in every position, including emergency goalkeeper, and became a hugely popular character at the club, famous for his flowing locks. He made 349 starts and scored 63 goals for the Robins during an eight-season spell at Whaddon Road.

Jordan made his debut on the opening day of the 1983/84 season in a 1-0 defeat at Sutton Coldfield Town. Wood was sacked as Cheltenham manager in December 1983, but John Murphy took over and led the side to an eighth placed finish. Jordan made 40 appearances and scored 12 goals during his first season with the Robins.

The following season saw Cheltenham win the Southern League title by two points from

Nick Jordan was one of Cheltenham's key players in their first season of Conference football.

season kicked off. He made his final Robins appearance against Yate Town in a 1-0 County Cup win and his final goals came against Taunton Town in the 8-0 FA Cup second qualifying round win, when he bagged a brace. He left after thirteen appearances that season and signed for Evesham United before returning to Moreton Town as player-boss.

His flowing locks may have turned grey with time, but the memories of his time with Cheltenham remain golden and he can often be seen cheering on the current Robins team from the stands at Whaddon Road.

Long-serving and hugely popular striker Dave Lewis has scored more goals for Cheltenham Town than anybody else and an incredible 53 of his 290 Robins goals came during his most prolific season in 1974/75.

David Dennis Lewis was born in Cheltenham on 8 August 1951 and started out in local football, turning out for St Marks and Cheltenham YMCA as a youngster and gaining representative honours with the Gloucestershire County Youth team for two seasons. He joined the Robins' youth side and made his first team debut as a sixteen-year-old in a Midland Floodlit Cup tie during the 1967/68 season. He spent periods on trial with Swindon Town and Bristol City, but Bob Etheridge signed him permanently for Cheltenham in August 1970.

He made his League debut on the first day of the 1970/71 campaign against Folkestone at Whaddon Road. His first goal arrived against Tonbridge in a 2-2 draw and he was soon attracting the interest of Football League clubs with his trademark clinical finishing. He

remained at Cheltenham and was the top scorer for nine consecutive seasons. He was top of the Southern League goalscoring charts in 1974/75 with 33 of his club-record 53 goals coming in the league. In January 1975, he scored five goals in an 8-0 triumph over Wellingborough Town. His remarkable total of goals that season came from 56 games and included five hat-tricks, a feat never bettered by a Robins striker.

He was one of the key figures in Cheltenham's 1976/77 Southern League promotion team, but then spent two years at Gloucester City after being controversially released by Alan Grundy in 1979, a move that he once described as the biggest disappointment of his career. He was the Tigers' top scorer in both seasons and also appeared in the Southern League Cup final. Before departing to City, Lewis endeared himself to the Robins faithful with a cameo appearance in goal against Altrincham in a 2-1 FA Trophy success which earned him the nickname 'the flying pig'. Lewis scored 30 goals in the Trophy including a hat-trick against Bath City to secure Cheltenham a 4-3 win when they trailed 3-1 with seven minutes remaining. He scored another treble against Bromsgrove in the next round and three years later he scored four against Bath in a 7-1 win. He returned to Cheltenham in July 1982 and helped the Robins to the Southern League Midland Division title in 1983. His overall Southern League record was 205 goals in 391 games.

After a spell as player-manager at St Marks, he became Robins reserve-team boss in 1984. He spent spells as caretaker first-team boss following the resignations of John Murphy in 1988 and 1991, and briefly managed the club following the sacking of Jim Barron in November 1989. Under his guidance, the club survived relegation from the Conference in 1990/91.

He left Whaddon Road and after a brief spell at St Marks, he became manager of Bishop's Cleeve, managing the first-team for seven seasons. He can still be seen helping out behind the bar at Kayte Lane and has been a Cleeve stalwart, earning the title 'best bloke in football' from a national football magazine.

Above: Dave Lewis converts a penalty.

Right: Cheltenham Town's record goalscorer Lewis on the ball.

One of Cheltenham's true legends; as well as being the club's leading marksman, Lewis is second only to Roger Thorndale in the all-time appearance makers. He was rewarded for his sterling service with a testimonial match against Aston Villa in 1992, which drew a crowd of over 2,000.

Lewis has worked for Smiths Industries since leaving school and is now assistant quality manager. He appeared at Whaddon Road in July 2006, making a cameo appearance for the Cheltenham Town Legends XI who took on the Robins' first team to mark Jamie Victory's glorious decade at the club.

Belfast-born Grant McCann was one of Cheltenham Town's key players as they regained their place in Coca-Cola League One with their second play-off success in May 2006.

McCann started his career as a trainee at West Ham United, making four substitute appearances on loan at Scottish club Livingston and was then loaned to Notts County. He contracted a virus that caused him to lose over a stone in weight and he returned to his Premiership parent club after three appearances for the Magpies.

In November 2000, McCann joined Cheltenham Town in a long-term loan deal, remaining at Whaddon Road for the remainder of the 2000/01 season. Performing at either left-back or on the left of midfield, he impressed with his attitude and some fine skills on the ball. He made his debut in a 2-0 home defeat by Rochdale on 21 October 2000 and went on to make 27 League starts and 3 substitute appearances during his first spell at Whaddon Road. He scored a free-kick at Barnet in a 2-2 draw, the first goal against Brighton and Hove Albion in a memorable 3-1 win over the eventual champions at Whaddon Road and also crafted a fine solo effort against Southend on the final day of the season in a 2-0 win.

He returned to Upton Park at the end of Cheltenham's campaign and made his senior debut as a late substitute in the Hammers' final match of the season at Middlesbrough, before signing a new deal with the East London club. He was involved in the early part of the Hammers' 2001/02 season as Glenn Roeder took over from Harry Redknapp as the Hammers' boss. He went on as a substitute in three matches, including the first two clashes of the season against Liverpool and Leeds United. He also went on at Blackburn on 14 October 2001, but he scored an own goal in a 7-1 defeat and faded from the first team scene at Upton Park.

McCann came close to signing for Grimsby Town, but joined Cheltenham's League One challenge, again on loan, during the 2002/03 season. He was recalled by West Ham after eight league appearances, but soon agreed a permanent move to Whaddon Road in January 2003 for a club record fee of £50,000. He was boss Bobby Gould's first signing for Cheltenham Town. McCann's arrival coincided with an upturn in performances and he scored a trademark free-kick against Port Vale in a 2-1 victory at Vale Park. He scored 6 goals in 27 League outings that term, but was unable to prevent the club suffering relegation at the end of the season. Having previously been used on the left, McCann began to shine in the centre of midfield. He added four Northern Ireland caps to his total during the 2002/03 season, leaving him with seven and making him the second player to win international caps while at Cheltenham after his good friend and Northern Ireland colleague Michael Duff.

Northern Ireland international Grant McCann is one of the most technically proficient players to represent Cheltenham Town.

McCann scored eight League goals, including two penalties, during the 2003/04 season as Cheltenham finished fourteenth back in the basement division. He scored a late winner against Kidderminster Harriers in a 2-1 league victory and scored another winner at Macclesfield Town as Cheltenham won by the same scoreline. However, his most spectacular strike came in an FA Cup third round tie against Fulham at Loftus Road. His long-range swerving drive deceived Edwin van der Sar in the Fulham goal and nestled in the back of the net to spark wild celebrations in the fifth minute. Louis Saha equalised eight minutes later and scored a last minute winner, but it was a tremendous effort from John Ward's team in their first ever match against a Premiership club.

McCann scored 4 goals in 39 League matches during the 2004/05 season as Cheltenham finished fourteenth for the second year running. His best strike was a vicious curling drive against Swansea in a 1-1 draw at the Vetch Field. He scored the only goal in a 1-0 win at Bury and was on target in a 4-1 win over Rushden and Diamonds at Whaddon Road. His considerable talent helped Cheltenham jump from a mid-table team to play-off winners at the end of

the 2005/06 season. He made 47 appearances and contributed 11 goals in all competitions as Cheltenham defeated Grimsby Town in the final at the Millennium Stadium in May 2006. Technically as good as any player to represent Cheltenham Town, McCann had made a total of 196 starts and 4 substitute appearances and scored 39 goals, many of which have been of the spectacular variety, by the end of the 2005/06 season.

McCann has also taken his total of international caps into double figures during his time at Cheltenham. His debut came in a 1-0 win over Malta in a 2001 World Cup qualifier and he appeared against Portugal and Estonia during the 2005/06 season. McCann won his twelfth cap for Northern Ireland in a 2-1 international friendly victory on 16 August 2006. He started the match in the centre of midfield in Helsinki, with former Robin Michael Duff joining the action from the bench as a substitute.

McCann's brother Ryan was at Glasgow Rangers as a youngster, before returning to Northern Ireland and representing Linfield. He spent a brief period on trial with Cheltenham during the summer of 2003.

Grant McCann tussles for the ball in midfield on his way to helping Cheltenham Town win promotion in 2006.

Jeff Miles
Goalkeeper, 1975-1980

Jeff Miles was a very popular and accomplished goalkeeper who joined the Robins from Gloucester City in 1975. Born just over the Welsh border in Caldicot, he played briefly for Cinderford Town before joining Newport County as an amateur in 1966 while employed as a bank clerk. He sampled reserve-team football before being loaned to Hereford United during the 1967/68 campaign. He helped them to knock County out of the Welsh FA Cup and subsequently returned to Somerton Park as cover for record appearance holder Len Weare. He was given his Football League debut in Newport's 1-0 win at home to Darlington in April 1968. He joined Gloucester in 1971 and succeeded Roy Jones as their first choice goalkeeper, moving to Whaddon Road during the summer before the 1975/76 season.

Miles made his Cheltenham debut in a 1-1 draw at AP Leamington on the opening day of the season. He made 47 appearances as Cheltenham finished fifth in Division One North of the Southern League. Miles went on to become the regular number one at Whaddon Road for five years. He was voted player of the year in 1975/76 – his first season at the club – and he was one of the key players in the side that won promotion back to the Southern League Premier Division the following year after a six-season absence. The Robins finished as runners-up to Worcester City, with 23 wins from their 38 matches and Miles appeared in 45 matches.

He was injured at the start of the 1977/78 season, giving back-up stopper Nigel Berry a run in the side. Between them, the two played in the club's record unbeaten run of 19 matches in all competitions. The run came to an end against Bedford Town on 24 September 1977 and Cheltenham went on to finish fourteenth in the Premier Division. Miles recovered from his injury and made 4 appearances, keeping 2 clean sheets.

Miles returned to be first choice in 1978/79 and Cheltenham were drawn away to the great Altrincham side who had held Tottenham Hotspur to a draw in the FA Cup in the third round for an FA Trophy first round tie. Miles and Berry were both unavailable, so record goalscorer Dave Lewis played in goal, and his legendary performance earned him the nickname 'The Flying Pig' as Cheltenham claimed a 2-1 win. Despite Lewis' heroics, Miles reclaimed the goalkeeper's jersey for the following match against Bridgend Town and Lewis resumed normal service up front with a brace in a 2-0 triumph.

After 172 appearances, including 133 Southern League outings, Miles left at the end of the 1979/80 season and rejoined Gloucester City, where he stayed for a further two seasons, along with Lewis, Dave Dangerfield and John Davies after a clearout by then-Robins boss Allan Grundy. He retired from football as work commitments gradually took over and he worked for the Abbey National building society in Aberdare.

Stylish midfielder Russell Milton joined Cheltenham as their remarkable success story began and he became a key player as the club established themselves in the Football League. Milton is a lifelong Arsenal fan and his all-time favourite player is Liam Brady. He started as a trainee at Highbury and played in the same reserve team as Paul Merson during his days as a Gunner, but he was given the opportunity to play professionally in Hong Kong at the age of just twenty-two. He turned down offers to play for Stoke City and Bury to move to the Far East, where both the lifestyle and the football were luxurious.

In Hong Kong, he played both alongside and against some top international players from a number of countries and also appeared for the invitation Hong Kong Select XI in representative games against leading teams from South America and Europe. He played for South China and also appeared in the same team as Brazilian internationals Socrates and Serginho during his time in Asia.

He returned to England in 1992 in search of a career and began training to be a teacher while playing for Dover Athletic in the Southern League Premier Division. Milton was a key member of the Dover team that claimed the Southern League Championship at the end of the 1992/93 season, when Cheltenham finished as runners-up. He remained at Dover for five seasons and won two England semi-professional caps during his time at the Crabble Athletic Ground, travelling to Finland and Norway on his international duty. His move to Cheltenham came about when he moved to Ledbury prior to the 1997/98 season and he chose to switch to Whaddon Road ahead of two other Conference clubs who had been chasing his signature.

Milton made his Cheltenham debut against Dover on the opening day of the 1997/98 season as they returned to the top flight of non-League football after a five-year absence in the Southern League. The £4,000 signing found himself on the losing side as his former club won 3-0. The Cheltenham team that day was: S. Book; M. Duff, C. Banks, J. Victory, S. Benton; K. Knight, L. Howells, B. Bloomer (D. Wright), R. Milton; D. Watkins, M. Crisp (J. Eaton).

To say that fortunes improved for both Milton and Cheltenham Town after that day at the Crabble would be a huge understatement. It was Milton who supplied the cross for Jason Eaton's FA Trophy winning goal and he also scored one and made another as Cheltenham stunned Championship club Burnley in their first ever FA Cup fourth round tie in 2002. His time at Cheltenham was hampered by injury, but he was still an influential figure and demonstrated time and time again why Arsenal signed him on as a youngster.

The Folkestone-born playmaker's first typically inch-perfect and decisive cross in Cheltenham colours came in a 3-2 win over Woking. Jamie Victory headed home Milton's perfectly delivered free-kick and the Robins were victorious over a side thought to be non-League giants with whom the likes of Cheltenham could only dream about rubbing shoulders.

Injury restricted Milton's appearances during Cheltenham's Conference title-winning season of 1998/99 to only twelve starts and thirteen substitute appearances. However, it was in the old Division Three that he began to make a real impression. He had been working as a corporate accounts assistant for Vodafone in Cheltenham and was one of the senior players in the Robins' squad who thought the Football League had escaped them. However, he was rejuvenated during Steve Cotterill's reign as boss and was given a chance to prove himself in the professional game. Full-time training clearly benefited Milton, who became noticeably fitter and sharper. He made his Football League debut against Brighton and Hove Albion in a 1-0 defeat at the Withdean Stadium on 25 September 1999.

He went on to make 108 Football League appearances for the Robins, scoring 14 League goals. His first came against Southend United

in what was his third League Two appearance and proved to be something of a turning point in Cheltenham's play-off chasing debut season in Division Three. The goal was deflected but Milton soon became a regular scorer, chalking up eight more in his first season in the full-time ranks. As well as his League strikes he scored a superb effort in the FA Cup defeat at Gillingham in a narrow 3-2 replay defeat at the Priestfield Stadium. He also scored the club's first goal in the Football League Trophy, stroking home a well placed shot in a 1-0 victory at Southend United. He featured in 38 of Cheltenham's 46 League matches and scored 11 goals in all competitions. He was named as the Supporters' Player of the Year, capping what was a memorable season and certainly his best in a Robins shirt.

The following year, Milton scored another outstanding FA Cup goal in a defeat, this time in a 3-1 reverse at Cardiff. He made 19 League

A delighted Russell Milton celebrates his historic FA Cup goal against Burnley in the 2-1 fourth round win in January 2002.

appearances during the 2000/01 season as Cheltenham finished ninth in League Two. He scored one goal in the League, hitting the fourth in a 4-2 win over Halifax Town.

It was third time lucky for Milton and Cheltenham in the 2001/02 FA Cup. Steve Cotterill once joked that he should send Milton on just for set pieces with a bucket of sand. Against Burnley, Milton scored a free-kick from the edge of the box and then put a great ball across for Julian Alsop to make it 2-0. He was also on target along with Hugh McAuley against Swindon Town in 2003 to earn Cheltenham their first win in what is now League One.

Milton's most familiar position during his Cheltenham career was on the left side of midfield, but he was also deployed in the middle. Following Graham Allner's departure during the 2002/03 season, Milton was recalled to the team by caretaker trio, Banks, Bloomer and Yates. He starred in the centre of the park at Cardiff's Ninian Park, pulling the strings as Cheltenham gave their fans renewed hope that they could climb clear of the bottom four. After Bobby Gould's arrival, Milton became a peripheral figure and he was released at the end of Cheltenham's first season in what is now League One.

Milton possessed a talent rarely seen in the lower-league game and he will be remembered as one of the most elegant and naturally gifted players ever to grace Whaddon Road. After leaving Cheltenham, he signed for Bath City in the Southern League Premier Division, but has since hung up his boots. He was one of the former Cheltenham favourites who graced the Whaddon Road pitch once more during Jamie Victory's testimonial match in July 2006. Still based in Cheltenham, he has set up a soccer school for kids, Premier Sports Coaching, which he runs in association with Arsenal FC and he can also be heard on BBC Radio Gloucestershire, as the Robins' expert analyst for away matches.

John Murphy was born locally and played for Bishop's Cleeve, Forest Green Rovers and Cinderford Town before joining Cheltenham Town in August 1974. He was an athletic right-back or central defender who made 220 appearances and scored 7 goals during his first spell, and was a regular in the side that won promotion from the Southern League Division One North in 1976/77.

He made his Robins debut in a 1-0 win over Bedworth United on 17 August 1974. He played 19 matches during his debut season. He made 48 appearances the following year as Cheltenham finished fifth in the Southern League Division One North and he found the net for the first time on the opening day of the season at AP Leamington in a 1-1 draw. He scored his second Robins goal in a 2-0 Welsh Cup first round first leg win over Barry Town on 27 August 1975.

He made 49 appearances during the 1976/77 season and scored another 3 goals, against Clevedon Town, Barry Town and Milton Keynes, as Cheltenham finished as runners-up to Worcester City in Division One North and claimed a place in the Premier Division. The consistent Murphy made 54 appearances and scored 1 goal during the club's first campaign in the Southern Premier Division as they finished fourteenth. He reached the half century again during the 1978/79 season making 50 appearances and scoring 1 goal as Cheltenham finished eighteenth and the League was reorganised placing Cheltenham in the Midland Division for the following campaign.

After a brief spell playing up north, Murphy made his comeback appearance against Milton Keynes on 21 August 1982 and Cheltenham took the Midland Division title by one point from Sutton United to rejoin the newly reformed Premier Division. He made 57 appearances that season, with only Chris Ogden making as many. Murphy made another 45 appearances during the 1983/84 season, taking his Robins career total to 322. He scored his final two goals against Stourbridge on 7 March 1984 and against Forest Green Rovers in the County Cup semi-final defeat.

John Murphy was appointed as manager of Cheltenham Town on 18 December 1983 following the dismissal of Alan Wood and in his first season in football management he guided Cheltenham to the Southern League title and promotion to the top flight of non-League football. He made 26 appearances during the 1984/85 season that saw Cheltenham win the Southern League Premier Division title. He remained in charge until 1 October 1988 when he quit after an embarrassing 3-0 defeat at the hands of Gloucester City in an FA Cup second qualifier. Jim Barron took over, but he departed on 16 October 1990 and Murphy briefly stepped back into the hot seat. Murphy made a total of 354 appearances for Cheltenham and scored 10 goals.

Wonderfully talented forward Tony Naylor signed for Cheltenham Town in the summer of 2001 and helped the club achieve promotion for the first time as a Football League club and surpass their previous best run in the FA Cup. Manchester-born Naylor arrived at Whaddon Road with a scoring record of roughly one in every three matches during his twelve previous seasons in the Football League. His professional career began when Crewe Alexandra paid £20,000 to sign him from Northern Premier League Droylsden in 1989. He scored 45 goals in 122 appearances for Dario Gradi's men but Port Vale splashed out £150,000 for him in 1994. He spent five seasons in Division One before Vale were relegated at the end of season 1999/00. Naylor appeared for the Valiants in their LDV Vans Trophy final win over Brentford at the Millennium Stadium but after 71 League goals in 253 games for Vale, he turned down a new contract with the Potteries, club, prompting Steve Cotterill to step in with an offer for him to lead the Robins' forward line.

Naylor signed for Cheltenham on a 'Bosman' free after protracted negotiations with Cotterill, who saw him as the final link in his promotion puzzle. That proved to be justified as Naylor teamed up with Julian Alsop in a prolific 'little and large' partnership which yielded 44 goals, culminating in the play-off final triumph against Rushden & Diamonds at the Millennium Stadium. Naylor helped himself to 18 goals in his first campaign at Whaddon Road.

He endured something of a barren spell when he first arrived and was clearly lacking fitness, but he soon began to light up Whaddon Road with his deft touches, fantastic vision and clinical finishing. He scored his first goal for the club against Lincoln City in a 2-1 home victory on 5 October 2001. He found the net in a 3-1 home win over Exeter City and scored against Cambridge United in the Football League Trophy second round defeat. He then bagged a brace in a 6-1 FA Cup first round win over Kettering Town at Rockingham Road. He was on target again in the second round against Hinckley Town in a 2-0 victory and then scored a brace to shock Oldham Athletic of League One as League Two Cheltenham Town reached the last thirty-two of the FA Cup for the first time in their history.

Back in the League a run of four goals in three games over the Christmas period, including a brace at York City in a 3-1 win, had helped establish Cheltenham as genuine promotion contenders. Naylor helped Cheltenham shock Championship side Burnley in the fourth round of the FA Cup but they were knocked out after a brave performance against West Bromwich Albion at The Hawthorns in the last sixteen. Cheltenham missed out on automatic promotion on the final day of the season, but Naylor was prominent as the Robins defeated Hartlepool in the play-off semi-finals to reach

Right: Tony Naylor takes on Norwich
City in Cheltenham's 3-0 League
Cup victory at Carrow Road in
2002.

the final at Cardiff's Millennium Stadium. Naylor partnered Alsop in attack against Rushden and Diamonds. He set up Alsop for Cheltenham's second goal and they went on to win 3-1 and claim their place in League One for the first time.

In his second season at Cheltenham, Naylor scored eight goals, notably coming off the bench at Wycombe to net a dramatic equaliser. He scored Cheltenham's first goal in Division Two – a late leveller at Barnsley – and he also proved the catalyst for the 3-0 win over Blackpool in the penultimate game of the season as Cheltenham's brave battle against relegation ended in disappointment at Notts County.

He netted a total of 18 League goals in 74 outings for the Robins before being released at the end of the 2002/03 season. He made 449 career Football League appearances and scored 134 goals between 1989 and 2003. Naylor is without doubt one of the most gifted players ever to pull on the red and white shirt. He was coming to the end of fantastic career when he signed for the club, but he still had time to entertain the fans and help Cheltenham into uncharted territory.

D avid Norton may have spent only one season at Whaddon Road, but the big-hearted player made a huge impact during the 1998/99 Conference Championship-winning season and left an indelible mark on the club.

Born in Cannock on 3 March 1965, Norton's career began at Aston Villa, where he signed schoolboy forms at the age of eleven. He made his Villa debut on Saturday 19 January 1985 in a 3-0 win at Coventry City. He went on to make 54 starting first-team appearances between 1984 and 1988 as well as 3 further substitute outings. During that time Villa were promoted to the top flight and Norton played under the likes of Graham Taylor and Josef Venglos.

He played for Notts County, where he won another promotion, this time from the old third division to the second via the play-offs. Norton played in 15 of the Magpies' 46 matches as they finished third behind Bristol Rovers and Bristol City in the table. He found the net once that season – in a 4-2 away win over Preston North End. County overcame Bolton Wanderers and Tranmere Rovers in the play-offs to seal a place in what is now the Championship.

The stocky right-back or midfielder then made 157 appearances for Hull City, including a spell as club captain and he scored seven goals for the Tigers. He then turned out for Northampton Town, making 89 appearances before joining Hereford, where he was also skipper, but he left Edgar Street fearing that his playing career was over.

The former England Youth International played alongside another future Cheltenham player John Brough in the Hereford side that was relegated to the Conference on the last day of the 1996/97 season after Brighton's great escape act. During Hereford's first term back in non-League football Norton began as captain, but injury ended his season prematurely and he left the club. He was told by two surgeons that he should retire, but he refused to give up and battled back to fitness despite having a metal plate inserted in his leg.

Steve Cotterill snapped him up on a free transfer in the summer of 1998 and Norton had only one thing on his mind; to win a Conference winners' medal and help elevate Cheltenham into the Football League. It would go some way towards erasing the painful memories he was

Opposite: David Norton bursts through against Southport in 1998.

Right: Norton Competes against Dover during the 1998/99 Conference title-winning season.

left with after his time at Edgar Street. He made his debut in a 2-1 defeat by Welling United on 15 August 1998. The Cheltenham team that day was: S. Book; M. Duff, C. Banks, J. Brough, J. Victory; D. Norton (K. Knight), L. Howells, B. Bloomer, R. Milton (C. Walker); J. Eaton, N. Grayson. Sub not used: J. Smith.

What followed was one of the most amazing stories in Cheltenham's history. Norton was an instrumental component in Cheltenham's Championship success. He played arguably with more passion, determination and will to win than any other player to represent the club. Travelling down from his home in Nottingham up to three times a week, Norton made 46 appearances for the club, with a further 3 as a substitute. He found the net on three occasions, the first in a 2-1 success at Forest Green Rovers that earned Cotterill's team their first win of the season. He was also on target in the 3-0 home victory over Southport and fired one of the best goals of the season in a 2-2 draw at Yeovil Town. He hit the winning penalty in the memorable FA Trophy shoot-out triumph at Stevenage Borough, but Cheltenham missed out on a second trip to Wembley Stadium in two years,

losing out to Geoff Chapple's Kingstonian over two legs in the last four.

Unfortunately, Norton had taken an insurance pay out and was unable to join Steve Cotterill's men in their Third Division adventure. He turned down the offer of a coaching role at Cheltenham and decided to extend his non-League career and moved to Yeovil Town for a brief spell.

He set up his own leisurewear business 'Pro-Nort' and was soon co-manager of Forest Green with old Aston Villa pal Nigel Spink. The pair guided the club to an FA Trophy final at the ground where Norton's career started – Villa Park – where they were beaten 1-0 by Canvey Island. He moved on to Gainsborough Trinity and then Tamworth, who he helped win the Southern League Premier Division title in 2002/03 before joining Nuneaton Borough as their assistant manager. He was appointed manager of Grantham in February 2004, but resigned following a 4-2 defeat at home to Shepshed Dynamo in the FA Cup. Norton then moved to Stafford Rangers in October 2004 as player/assistant manager but left at the start of the 2005/06 season.

Defender, 1962-1966, 1967-1973

Yorkshireman Ronnie Radford shot to national stardom with his wonderful FA Cup strike for Hereford United against Newcastle United in 1972. Radford's defining moment became one of the most memorable goals in the history of the world's premier domestic knockout competition and came after he had spent seven seasons with Cheltenham Town.

Born in South Elmshall, South Yorkshire in July 1943, Radford spent the 1959/60 season as an amateur at Sheffield Wednesday under coach Maurice Lindle. He then spent a year as a professional with Leeds United from October 1961, where he was reunited with Lindley and played under manager Don Revie. He was sent a telegram telling him that Cheltenham wanted to sign him and he joined the Robins as a semi-professional in the summer of 1962. He moved down to Gloucestershire and started up his own carpentry and joinery business. The club had just been relegated from the Southern

League Premier Division and Radford was among a number of young signings made by Scottish manager Arch Anderson, who was in charge at Whaddon Road for a second spell between 1961 and 1965. He was on £12 a week at Cheltenham and made his Robins debut in a 1-1 draw with Margate, quickly establishing himself in the old-fashioned left-half position. He became an important member of the side that claimed promotion back to the Premier Division in 1963/64. He was ever-present during that season and remained at Cheltenham until the summer of 1966, when he switched to Rugby Town.

After suffering relegation at Rugby and just one season away from Cheltenham, he was brought back to Whaddon Road by Bob Etheridge, who took over as Robins boss in 1966 and remained at the helm until 1973. Radford featured at right-back in a Cheltenham team renowned for its attacking flair and entertaining football. He was named as Player of the Year at the end of the 1966/67 season. Cheltenham finished fourth in a very strong Premier Division during the 1967/68 season and he helped the club reach the League Cup final a year later. He gained representative honours during his time with Cheltenham. Radford departed for a second time to join Football League club Newport County for £1,500 in June 1971.

He made his League debut at the age of twenty-six and was named as the Somerton Park club's Player of the Year at the end of his first season. He scored 7 goals in 63 appearances for the Welsh club. His life changed forever when he was signed by Hereford boss John Charles for £1,000 in July 1971 and scored 'that' goal past Newcastle United goalkeeper and Northern Ireland international Ian McFaul for the non-League minnows to send the First Division giants tumbling out of the FA Cup in February 1972. The two sides had played out a 2-2 draw at St James' Park, but Radford's goal helped the Bulls win the replay 2-1 and reach the fourth round. The Magpies had taken the lead through Malcolm Macdonald, but Radford's goal levelled the scores and Ricky George scrambled home

Ronnie Radford (right) with his friend and former Cheltenham colleague Gerald Horlick.

a winner in extra time. Hereford became the first non-League side to defeat a top flight club since 1949 and they went through to round four, where they lost to West Ham United after another replay. The Newcastle match was screened live on BBC television and the thirty-yard screamer along with John Motson's commentary has become synonymous with FA Cup giant-killing acts. A mass pitch invasion followed Hereford's heroics, but Radford made a swift exit to the changing rooms. He was presented with a rose bowl to mark his achievements at Hereford and was with the club as they joined the Football League and won promotion from the fourth division at the first attempt at the end of the 1972/73 season.

Radford's career wound down at Worcester City, where he arrived as player-manager in July 1974. He moved to Bath City five months later, but an achilles tendon injury ended his playing career and he returned to Yorkshire in 1977 after sixteen years living in Cheltenham. He had a brief coaching spell at Ossett Albion, but returned to his old trade as a joiner. He built himself the house that he and his wife Ann moved into. Radford played 318 matches for the Robins and scored 28 goals. He refers to his time at the club as 'special' and his favourite Cheltenham goal came against Cambridge United in a 5-2 win. He was also proud to set up four goals in an 8-2 win over Yeovil Town and defeat a strong Wimbledon side 2-0 as Joe Gadston scored both goals. Radford has stayed in touch with many of his former Robins teammates including Joe Gadston, Gerald Horlick, Roger Thorndale and Willie Ferns, and he now lives in the village of Kirkhamgate, near Wakefield.

Striker, 1949-1951

Hard-as-nails centre forward Roy Shiner is rated as one of the leading marksmen to represent Cheltenham Town. Born in Ryde, Isle of Wight in November 1924, Shiner joined Cheltenham from Hampshire League club Ryde Sports in February 1948. He started out in the reserve team at Whaddon Road, but made his full debut against Gillingham on 17 September 1949 in a 3-1 defeat.

Shiner became one of the most feared strikers in the Southern League over the next three seasons and he enjoyed a particularly productive campaign in 1950/51, hitting 37 goals in the Southern League and 46 in total. He added five more goals in friendly matches against Portsmouth and Southampton. He followed up this prolific campaign with 22 goals in 26 matches a year later and it was only a matter of time before he began to attract attention from professional clubs. He made his final Cheltenham appearance in a 1-0 friendly defeat against Cardiff City on 12 December 1951. His final competitive appearance was a 5-1 win over Gravesend and Northfleet four days earlier.

First Division club Huddersfield Town paid £1,250 for his services later that month. Shiner's fee failed to break the club's record transfer received as Peter Rushworth had joined

Leicester City for £1,350 two weeks earlier. Shiner was a success in the full-time ranks, moving on to Hull City from Sheffield Wednesday for £5,000 in November 1959.

He had made his debut for the Owls on 20 August 1955 and spent the next four years at Hillsborough. He scored 33 goals in 42 League appearances for Wednesday during the 1955/56 season as they won the Division Two title and claimed a place in the top flight. He scored a total of 96 goals in 160 appearances for the Sheffield club and played his final match for the Owls on 26 September 1959.

He scored 8 goals in 22 League outings for the Tigers prior to rejoining Cheltenham in July 1961. He played up front in a struggling Cheltenham team and was named caretaker manager in September 1961 when Tommy Cavanagh departed after a brief spell in the hotseat. Arch Anderson was reappointed as manager after an earlier spell in charge from 1953 to 1958 and Shiner left Whaddon Road in January 1962. His final appearance was a 4-2 defeat at Cambridge City, where he scored both of Cheltenham's goals. He finished with 59 goals from 103 Southern League games for Cheltenham and scored six hat-tricks in his overall Robins goal haul of 79.

Jimmy Smith
Striker, 1992-1999

Jimmy Smith arrived at Whaddon Road in 1992 with a reputation as a prolific marksman and the wee Scotsman certainly did not disappoint the expectant Robins faithful. When he departed at the end of the Conference title-winning 1998/99 campaign, he was the second highest scorer in Cheltenham Town's history behind the great Dave Lewis.

Smith was born in Johnstone, Scotland and he started out playing schools football in Glasgow. His achievements attracted the attention of St Mirren and he signed forms at the Premier Division side. He was deemed too small to succeed at St Mirren and at the age of sixteen he wrote to Torquay United asking for a trial. The laid back Smith said the primary reason for choosing the Devon club was his liking for going on holiday there! On his way from Strathclyde to Devon, his father's old Ford Cortina broke down near Warrington and Smith was given £100 and told to find his own way to Torquay. Smith eventually arrived in Devon and immediately impressed at Plainmoor. He was taken on as a trainee, making his reserve-team debut at seventeen. He was called up to the senior side at eighteen and offered a two-year full-time contract. His room-mate at Torquay was a youthful Lee Sharpe, who progressed to play for Manchester United and England. Smith made his first appearance at Wembley Stadium in the 1989 Sherpa Vans trophy final, where the Gulls were beaten 4-1 by Bolton Wanderers before 56,000 fans. He made a total of 45 League appearances for Torquay, scoring 5 goals and playing in the same team as current Robins physiotherapist, Ian Weston, and another ex-Robin, Paul Hirons, at Plainmoor. Just as he was beginning to make a name for himself in the south-west, he sustained a serious knee injury which sidelined him for eight months. After so long out of action he was unable to regain a place in the team and was released in 1990.

Smith joined Southern League side Salisbury City and won the Southern League Golden Boot at the end of his first season in Wiltshire, racking up 45 goals. He began the next season in similarly prolific form and after adding another 24 goals to his City tally, he was snapped up by Cheltenham, initially on loan, but Lindsay Parsons soon paid £5,000 to Salisbury for Smith.

He made his Robins debut at Barrow in a 0-0 draw on 15 February 1992 and scored his first Cheltenham goals in a 3-1 win at Slough ten days later, bagging a brace. He made 16 appearances during his first season at Whaddon Road, but his 6 goals could not prevent Cheltenham suffering relegation from the Conference. However, his consistent scoring ensured that the Robins would be flying high throughout their five-year spell back in the Southern League.

He top scored in the 1992/93 season with 30 goals in 47 appearances when Cheltenham finished as runners-up to Dover Athletic. Dover had offered Cheltenham £10,000 for Smith in 1992, but the move never materialised. He also had opportunities to join Gloucester City, but he remained loyal to the Robins. The goals continued to flow for Smith as the Robins ended

Scotsman Jimmy Smith is Cheltenham's second highest goalscorer of all time.

second in 1994 and 1995. He scored 15 goals in 45 appearances during the 1993/94 season and 24 goals in 48 appearances the following year.

Smith had already struck up a lethal partnership with Jason Eaton and the pair netted over 50 goals between them during the 1995/96 campaign as the Robins ended up in third spot. Smith claimed 31 and passed his century of goals for the club, and Eaton hit 24 for Chris Robinson's side. Smith added 14 more to his total during the 1996/97 season as Cheltenham regained their Conference status. Due to the fine form of Eaton and new signing Dale Watkins, Smith was often used as a wide man by boss Steve Cotterill in the Conference, but he continued to chip in with vital goals and added 8 to

his impressive total from 32 appearances. After joining the action from the bench for his second Wembley outing, Smith won the free-kick that led to Eaton's FA Trophy-winning goal against Southport on 17 May 1998. He scored twice during his final season at the club in 1998/99, as Cheltenham claimed the Conference title. He put away a high pressure late penalty to earn Cheltenham a 3-3 draw with Hayes and his last goal was in a 5-0 Gloucestershire Senior Cup win over Cinderford Town.

Smith could often be seen working behind the bar underneath the main stand at Whaddon Road to supplement his earnings as a semi-professional footballer. He drove a 'vintage' silver Renault that was supplied by club director Colin Farmer after

Smith had succeeded in a goalscoring challenge. Smith finished with 131 goals from his 275 starts and is undoubtedly one of the best finishers the club has seen. One of his favourite goals was a stunning strike against Gloucester City at Christmas 1992 in a 4-0 for the Robins.

After his release from Whaddon Road, Smith signed for Gloucester and he scored 19 goals in 40 starts for the Tigers. He made a brief return to former club Salisbury, before heading back to his native Scotland. He moved back down south last year and after a brief spell at Brislington, he joined Bishops Cleeve as a player, before becoming part of manager Paul Collicutt's coaching staff at Kayte Lane. He helped the club reach the Southern League for the first time ahead of the 2006/07 season with a runners-up finish in the Hellenic League Premier Division.

Paul Tester

Skilful winger Paul Tester was twice Cheltenham's leading marksman in the 1980s and won the club's Player of the Year award in 1983 as the Robins won the Southern League Midland Division title. Born in Stroud, Tester attended Eastcombe Manor School and played locally for Chalford. He moved on to Shortwood United before arriving at Whaddon Road in January 1980 after a recommendation from Pat Casey to boss Allan Grundy.

Tester scored on his debut in a 2-0 win over King's Lynn on 12 March 1980. He made one further first-team appearance that season against Bedworth in a 1-0 defeat on 3 April. He made 38 appearances and scored 13 goals the following season as Cheltenham finished eighth in the Southern League Midland Division. He scored against Cambridge City in an opening day defeat on 16 August 1980 and bagged a brace against Barry Town in a 3-0 home win on 26 November.

He played in more matches than anyone else at the club during the 1981/82 season, making 54 appearances and scoring 10 goals as Cheltenham finished sixteenth. He made 53 appearances during the 1982/83 season and topped the scoring charts with 25 as Cheltenham won the Midland Division championship, finishing one point ahead of runners-up Sutton United. He scored a hat-trick against Redditch United on 11 March 1983 during a spell of 7 goals in 4 matches to help Cheltenham clinch the title. His final goal for the club came in a 2-0 win over Forest Green Rovers on 2 May of that year and his final appearance for the Robins was a goalless draw against Wellingborough on 7 May, the last day of the 1982/83 season.

Tester scored a total of 49 goals in 147 matches for Cheltenham and was sold to Shrewsbury Town for a then–club record fee

of £10,000 in May 1983 and quickly became an influential figure for the Shropshire club; starring in Shrewsbury's Welsh Cup triumphs in two consecutive seasons and also helping them reach the fifth round of the League Cup in 1986/87.

After 12 goals in 98 old Second Division outings for Shrewsbury, Hereford secured his signature for £10,000 in August 1988 after a successful loan spell. He played against Manchester United for the Bulls in the 1989/90 FA Cup and helped Hereford win the Welsh Cup for the first time later that season.

Tester briefly returned to Cheltenham on loan from Worcester City, who he had joined on a free transfer along with Colin Robinson, in November 1991, making a further six Conference appearances for the Robins. He was reunited with Robinson at Bridgnorth Town in March 1993 before moving on to Knighton Town in July 1995 and then becoming Chasetown's player-coach a year later. Tester now lives in Cheslyn Hay and has been working as a warehouse manager for Frans Maar, a freight forwarding company in Brownhills.

M artin Thomas joined Cheltenham at the start of the 1993/94 campaign, linking up with his old Bristol Rovers teammate and Robins' boss Lindsay Parsons. The Welsh goalkeeper was born in 1959 in Senghennydd and arrived at Whaddon Road with nearly 500 Football League appearances to his name. He was vastly experienced among a very youthful squad including the likes of teenagers Simon Cooper, Andy Tucker, Christer Warren and Paul Mortimore.

Thomas began his career as a trainee at Rovers making 162 League appearances, before spells with Newcastle United and Birmingham City. He was in goal for the Magpies the day Paul Gascoigne made his debut for the club and also played alongside Peter Beardsley and Kevin Keegan while at St James' Park. He made one appearance for Wales in a European Championships qualifier away to Finland in 1986, which finished 1-1. He also enjoyed loan spells at Cardiff City, Tottenham Hotspur,

Southend United, Middlesbrough, Crystal Palace and Aston Villa during a widely travelled professional career. During his time at St Andrews, he was a teammate of former Robins midfielder Mark Yates and won the Leyland Daf Cup at Wembley in 1992 with the Blues.

He made his Robins debut against Chelmsford City in August 1993 and soon began to show his international class at Whaddon Road. He was superb throughout his first season, when he was deservedly named as Supporters' Player of the Year for a series of fine displays between the sticks. Cheltenham missed out on promotion to the Conference, finishing second behind Farnborough Town. He made 52 appearances in all competitions during the 1993/94 campaign, keeping 17 clean sheets. He missed a 4-2 FA Cup fourth qualifying round defeat at Bath City and 1-0 home League defeat to Trowbridge Town.

He was again outstanding during the 1994/95 season when the Robins agonisingly missed out on promotion once again, finishing second for the third successive year, this time to Hednesford Town. Parsons' exciting side also set a new club record for points accumulated during a season (86). Thomas made 41 appearances during a campaign that also saw Cheltenham go 20 matches unbeaten from Boxing Day 1994 to 22 April 1995. The club to end the run was Burton Albion, who had been the final team to defeat Cheltenham before the impressive streak began.

'Thommo' was a consummate professional and was extremely popular among the rest of the squad. He went on to make 103 appearances for the Robins before retiring in 1995. He started the first ten matches of the 1995/96 season, but his final appearance for Cheltenham was an FA Cup third qualifying round defeat at Forest Green Rovers in September 1995. He sat on the bench for the following three matches against Rushden and Diamonds, Weston-super-Mare and Gresley Rovers before calling time on his playing days.

Now a specialist goalkeeping coach as well as a qualified physiotherapist, Thomas has since been involved with the England under-21 and full squads, deputising for Ray Clemence as the goalkeeping coach for the national set-up throughout the reign of Sven Goran Eriksson.

Thomas was in the main stand at Burton Albion cheering on his old mates as Cheltenham won promotion to the Conference in May 1997 with a 0-0 draw at Eton Park. He will be remembered as a great ambassador and arguably the finest goalkeeper to represent the club.

Defender, 1960-1975

Roger Thorndale has played more games for Cheltenham Town than anyone else and his long-standing record of 702 first-team appearances is unlikely ever to be threatened.

A local lad, Thorndale joined the club as a fifteen-year-old in 1955 and started out in the Colts side. He soon graduated through to the reserves and made his senior debut in the Southern League at wing-half in a goalless draw against Kettering Town on 18 April 1960. The Cheltenham Town line-up that day was: Gourlay, Thorndale, Farrell, Dunlop, Hyde, Dunn, Scott, Fowler, Cleland, Coldray, Burder.

The hard-tackling Thorndale soon became a fixture in the Robins' side and settled in at right-back, where he was respected for his defensive abilities and awareness. During his first fourteen campaigns at Whaddon Road, Thorndale only managed three goals, one of which came in the Midland Floodlit Cup. That changed when he was nominated as the team's regular penalty taker in the 1970s and he finished his Robins career with a respectable 24 goals to his name. He remained as the spot kick taker until Dave Lewis came on to the scene and smashed all the club's scoring records.

Thorndale was awarded a testimonial in 1966, when a full strength Derby County side came to Whaddon Road. Such was the length of his service, he was handed a second testimonial eight years later when Hereford United took on an Invitation XI. His 500th appearance came in May 1970 when Dunstable Town were crushed 6-0 and Thorndale was presented with a silver salver to mark the unique achievement. Thorndale's only competitive appearance on a Football League ground was in the FA Cup tie at Brighton in 1970, which the Seagulls won 4-0.

A superb team spirit was created at Cheltenham during the 1960s and 70s and the effervescent character of Thorndale was a key ingredient in the dressing room unity. He experienced promotion to the Southern Premier Division with the Robins in 1963/64 and relegation twice in 1961/62 and 1968/69. He was also on the losing side in the Southern League Cup final in 1968/69. His Cheltenham Town career spanned eight different Robins managers: Ron Lewin (1958-60), Peter Donnelly (1960-61), Tommy Cavanagh (1961), Arch Anderson (1961-1965), Harold Fletcher (1965-1966), Bob Etheridge (1966-1973), Willie Penman (1973-1974) and Dennis Allen (1974-1979). His final appearance was on Boxing Day 1975 in a 2-1 defeat against Worcester City at St Georges Lane – his 523rd League outing. The Cheltenham team that day was: Miles, Thorndale, Lailey, Davies, Murphy, Paterson, Gough, Casey, Lewis, Hehir, Dangerfield. Sub: Collicutt.

After retiring from playing, Thorndale managed the club's reserve side in the West Midland League, guiding them to the Division One Cup in 1978. He also had a brief spell as caretaker boss when Terry Paine resigned in 1979, before a stint as manager of local club Smiths Athletic. He made a hugely popular appearance on the Whaddon Road pitch last summer during 'legends' day' to mark the launch of the Robins Trust. Thorndale stood proudly alongside fellow club legends such as Gerald Horlick, Alan Jefferies, Jimmy Smith, Jason Eaton, Lee Howells and Mark Boyland. Thorndale's incredible consistency and unerring loyalty establish him firmly as one of Cheltenham Town's true greats and his massive contribution to the club will never be forgotten.

Jamie Victory

Defender/midfield, 1996-

When Jamie Victory first appeared for Cheltenham Town in a friendly at Cinderford Town ten years ago, he was looking to put himself in the shop window and earn a quick move back into the Football League. He was then a twenty-year-old who had suffered the disappointment of being told he was surplus to requirements at West Ham United – where he was once named Young Hammer of the Year – and AFC Bournemouth. What has come to pass during his ten years at the club has been hard to take in for fans of Cheltenham Town and Victory himself. 'It's like a fairytale story,' the Hackney-born left-back said while considering his glorious decade at Whaddon Road. 'I came to Cheltenham to keep fit and play some football while I found another League club. That didn't happen, but I was able to play in the League with Cheltenham which was unbelievable.'

After 16 Football League appearances and 1 goal for Bournemouth during the 1996/97

season, Victory was released by the Dean Court club. He made his debut for the Robins in a Southern League Premier Division match against Sittingbourne in August 1996, which was watched by 703 fans. His first goal came against King's Lynn in a 2-0 victory in Norfolk as Cheltenham started their Southern League Premier Division campaign with three consecutive wins.

It soon became obvious that Victory was capable of playing at a much higher level, but to many people's surprise he stayed at Cheltenham for the remainder of the 1996/97 season that finished with the first of four promotions he has been able to celebrate as a Robin. Victory and Cheltenham made an instant impression on their return to the Conference and he was the only player to start all 61 matches as Steve Cotterill's men shattered club records with a runners-up finish in the top tier of non-League football and an FA Trophy win at Wembley. 'It was not the best of games, but it was a great occasion,' Victory said of Cheltenham's 1-0 win over Southport in the final. 'Steve Cotterill is a winner and he came in and changed things around at the club, making it more professional on and off the pitch. It was a great time and he got the best out of everyone.'

Victory had scored the winning goal against Hayes at Whaddon Road in the second match of the 1997/98 season which secured their first three-point haul back in the Conference. He scored against Woking with a bullet header four days later when Cheltenham beat the non-League giants 3-2 and quickly began to establish themselves at the higher level. He scored one of his best goals for the club in a 4-1 defeat at Rushden and Diamonds in March 1998, weaving past several defenders and firing home a well-struck left-footed shot. Big-spending Diamonds' boss Brian Talbot tried to sign Victory, who was living in Rushden at the time, but he remained loyal to Cheltenham. His form for the Robins earned him an England Semi-Professional call-up and he made his international debut in a 2-1 win over Holland at Crawley Town's Broadfield Stadium in March 1998. He

Jamie Victory celebrates a goal with Tony Naylor during the 2001/02 promotion season.

he scored the historic goal, seven minutes into injury time. The goal has been officially credited to Michael Duff, who jumped with Victory to meet Keith Knight's free-kick and spark the wildest night of celebrations Whaddon Road has ever seen. 'I know I scored it,' Victory said. 'The ball came over and I headed it and there was so much relief that I scored and I just walked off. Duffo said to me he that he hadn't touched it and I know deep down that I scored.' Victory definitely scored Cheltenham's second goal on that most memorable of nights and he found the net on five other occasions as the title was won and Football League status was assured.

Life in the League began promisingly, with Victory forming a highly effective partnership with Russell Milton on the left as Cheltenham missed out on the play-offs on the final day of the 1999/00 season. He appeared in all 46 of the Robins' League matches during their first year as a full-time club and scored 4 goals in League Two. He scored a late winner in an excellent 2-1 win over automatic promotion-bound Northampton Town. Victory also hit the net with a header in the club's shock 2-1 League Cup first round second leg win, over Championship club Norwich City, at Whaddon Road in their debut in the competition.

Victory endured his toughest times the following summer after he tore a cruciate knee ligament in a 2-1 win over Torquay United and missed the next year of football. He said:

> I carried on playing for ten minutes, but when I went up for a header my knee gave way so I thought it was time to come off. It was a low, but it was my first injury and I had to relish the challenge of getting fit. I took it on the chin and came back a better player. There was no use in moping around. I let the surgeon do his work and then I had to do all the hard work in the gym and the training ground and get myself back. You have to remain positive at all times.

appeared at left-back as a substitute alongside fellow Robins Chris Banks, Dale Watkins, Lee Howells and Neil Grayson. The England team that day was: B. Stewart (Southport) (sub S. Cooksey – Hednesford Town); C. Banks (Cheltenham), M. Smith (Stevenage Borough), T. Ryan (Southport); D. Hooper (Kingstonian) (sub A. Comyn – Hednesford Town), L. Howells (Cheltenham), G. Butterworth (Rushden and Diamonds), B. Healy (Morecambe) (sub K. Betsy – Woking), M. Bradshaw (Halifax Town) (sub J. Victory – Cheltenham); N. Grayson (Cheltenham) (sub O. Pickard – Yeovil Town), D. Watkins (Cheltenham).

His second season at the club ended with the FA Trophy success, but things were to get even better a year later as Victory appeared in all forty-two games of Cheltenham's title-winning campaign to make League football a reality for a club that was on an amazing roll. The championship was secured with a 3-2 win over Yeovil on 22 April 1999 and Victory is adamant that

He came back as strong as ever and helped Cheltenham win an astonishing third promotion in six seasons and take their place in League One for the first time in 2002. He started 45 of their League matches and appeared in the 46 as a substitute as Cheltenham finished fourth and went up via the play-offs. He scored twice in a 2-2 draw at Rochdale and was on target in the first League win of the campaign against Carlisle at Whaddon Road. He also featured in rounds one to five of the record-breaking FA Cup run which saw the Robins reach the last sixteen for the first time in their history. He saw a header cleared off the line in the fifth round tie against West Bromwich Albion at The Hawthorns which Cheltenham lost 1-0 in front of 27,179 fans.

Cotterill's departure to Stoke and a season of struggle followed in 2002/03, but three years and some serious rebuilding later, Cheltenham and Victory were back in tier three and ready for their next challenge. During John Ward's first season as Cheltenham manager, Victory appeared in Cheltenham's first competitive match against a Premiership club when they were drawn to play Fulham at Loftus Road on 4 January 2004. Cheltenham took the lead in the fifth minute through Grant McCann, but Louis Saha's brace ended their hopes of an upset. One of the most impressive aspects of Cheltenham's performance was the way Victory dealt with dangerous French winger Steed Malbranque, who was enjoying a purple patch on the right for Chris Coleman's team.

He missed the second half of the 2005/06 promotion season, but recovered from the groin injury that sidelined him and was given a six-month contract to prove his fitness under a manager for whom he has the utmost respect. 'He is everything I want a manager to be,' Victory said of Ward. 'He talks to you, he is clever and tactically astute as well as a fantastic man manager. He is funny, but there is a serious

side to him and if I was to be a manager I'd like to be like him.'

A host of Cheltenham Town favourites turned out to mark Victory's testimonial in July 2006 when a Legends XI took on the Robins' first-team at Whaddon Road. The light-hearted contest finished in an entertaining 4-4 draw, but the day was all about Victory and was a fitting tribute to a player who has won more honours during his decade at Cheltenham than any other player in the history of the club.

At the start of the 2006/07 season, Victory had made 462 appearances for Cheltenham and scored 46 goals. He had made 248 Football League appearances – more than any other player and is undoubtedly one of the most talented, loyal and successful figures ever to grace the Whaddon Road pitch.

He played at the back for Cheltenham as they visited Wolverhampton Wanderers for an FA Cup first round tie during the 1987/88 season. Brett Angell gave Cheltenham the lead, but Steve Bull scored a hat-trick and Wolves won the tie 5-1. Vircavs played in 53 of Cheltenham's 61 matches during his second season, scoring 5 goals. He found the net against at Kettering Town in a 1-1 draw and also scored at Wealdstone in a 4-1 win. He netted the winner against Macclesfield Town in a 1-0 home success. His other two goals came against eventual champions Lincoln City in a thrilling 3-3 draw at Whaddon Road and in a 1-1 draw with Sutton United, also on Cheltenham's home patch.

Vircavs' consistent record continued in the 1988/89 season, when he played 42 matches and added 2 goals to his tally as Cheltenham finished sixteenth in the Conference. Cheltenham improved to end the 1989/90 season in eleventh place. Vircavs played 39 games and scored against Fisher Athletic in a 5-2 away win; he was also on target against Enfield in a 3-1 home victory.

Another 39 outings and 3 goals followed in the 1990/91 season as Vircavs passed 200 Cheltenham career appearances and the Robins finished sixteenth. Vircavs' final full season saw Cheltenham relegated from the upper echelon of the non-League pyramid. The defender made 42 appearances and scored 5 goals as Cheltenham dropped back into the Southern League. He made another 35 appearances in the Southern Premier Division before returning to Wycombe in March 1993 after making a total of 298 appearances for Cheltenham and scoring 20 goals. Many of his goals came from bullet headers and were often followed by outlandish celebrations much to the delight of the Whaddon Road faithful.

His strength, awareness and skill earned him an England semi-professional squad call-up in 1986 and he also represented the Middlesex Wanderers to confirm his status as one of the top defenders outside the Football League. Vircavs had originally been signed for Wycombe in

Anton Vircavs was an immensely popular centre half during the seven years he spent at Cheltenham Town after signing from Wycombe Wanderers for a then-club record fee of £5,000 just before the start of the 1986/87 season. Oxford-born Vircavs (pronounced 'Vic's house'), whose father was Latvian, became one of the stars of the Robins' first spell in the Conference, where they spent seven years between 1985 and 1992. An easy-going character, he was a rock at the heart of the Robins' defence as they tussled with the non-League elite.

Vircavs made 48 appearances in his first season at Whaddon Road, having made his Robins debut in August 1986 in a 3-1 win at Welling United. His first goal came in a 1-1 home draw with Runcorn on 10 January 1987 and Cheltenham finished eleventh in the Conference at the end of Vircavs' first campaign at the club.

Anton Vircavs (right) gets stuck in for Cheltenham in the club's first spell in the Conference.

1980 from Hellenic League club Pressed Steel at the age of nineteen. He made his return to the Buckinghamshire club in front of more than 7,000 fans at Adams Park and helped Wycombe win promotion to the Football League during his second spell, but he was dropped for the Chairboys' FA Trophy final against Runcorn, which they won 4-1 at Wembley. He played alongside Steve Guppy, who went on to play once for England and represented Leicester City in the Premiership and Keith Scott, who later went on to play at the top level for Swindon Town.

Vircavs made a total of 251 appearances for Wycombe, but turned down a professional contract at the age of thirty-two as he had already started his own heating business 'APV Boilers' and did not expect to be a first team regular at Adams Park. He spent one season with Witney Town and went on to manage Kidlington in the Hellenic League for a year. Now a keen golfer, Vircavs lives in Kidlington, north of Oxford, with his wife Helen and his three daughters.

Clive Walker

Winger/striker, 1997-1999

W ing wizard Clive Walker won an FA Trophy winners' medal and a Conference championship winners' medal during his two-year spell at Cheltenham Town. Born in Oxford on 25 June 1957, he may have been the wrong side of forty when he arrived at Cheltenham, but he was still able to treat the Whaddon Road crowd to some dazzling displays of skill and some spectacular goals. Walker was the most famous name in non-League football at that time and Robins boss Steve Cotterill pulled off a major coup by persuading the renowned FA Cup giant killer to join the club.

A former England schoolboy international, Clive joined Chelsea as a sixteen-year-old in 1973. He made his debut during the 1976/77 season and stayed at Stamford Bridge until 1984, making over 200 League and cup appearances in the top two divisions before joining Sunderland. He played in the 1985 League Cup final, in which he hit the post with a penalty and Sunderland lost 1-0 to Norwich

City. Spells with QPR, Fulham and Brighton and Hove Albion followed, including another Wembley appearance in the old Second Division play-off final which Brighton lost to Notts County. In all, Walker made 514 Football League appearances and scored 126 goals. One of the highlights of his professional career was scoring against Liverpool in the 1978 FA Cup third round as Chelsea won 4-2. He also scored a hat-trick for Sunderland against Manchester United in a 3-2 win in 1984 and scored a vital goal for Chelsea against Bolton Wanderers that kept the Blues up.

When his glittering full-time career came to an end, Walker spent four years at up-and-coming Conference club Woking. He joined the Cardinals in 1993 and scored 91 goals in four seasons at the Kingfield Stadium and helped Woking to three FA Trophy triumphs at Wembley in 1994, 1995 and 1997. He also helped the Surrey club achieve several giant killing acts including memorable victories over Millwall and Cambridge United. Woking also forced a draw against Premiership side Coventry City at Highfield Road in 1997 but they lost a replay 2-1.

Walker left Woking in the summer of 1997 and was in the process of signing for another club when he received a call from David Webb at Brentford asking if he'd take over as assistant manager under supremo Eddie May. Things did not work out for Walker and May at Griffin Park and he was out of work less than three months into his first foray into football management.

Cotterill was quick to phone his former Brighton teammate Walker and, after meeting with the Cheltenham boss, he was sufficiently impressed to join the Conference newcomers. He made his debut as a substitute at Slough Town in a 2-1 victory on 8 November 1997, much to the delight of the travelling Cheltenham fans among the crowd of 1,037. The Cheltenham team that day was: S. Book; M. Duff, C. Banks, M. Freeman, J. Victory; K. Knight (D. Wright), B. Bloomer, L. Howells, J. Smith (C. Walker); J. Eaton (M. Crisp), D. Watkins. He was not fully fit at the time, but his fitness quickly returned

Above: Clive Walker in action.

Opposite: Clive Walker celebrates the Robins' FA Trophy win on a Town Hall balcony in 1998.

even at his grand age and he scored a dramatic late winner in an FA Cup first round tie against Tiverton Town at Whaddon Road a week after his debut.

Walker's experience was crucial as Cheltenham progressed to the FA Trophy and although he failed to score a Wembley goal, the Robins beat Southport 1-0 thanks to Jason Eaton's seventy-ninth minute goal. It was Walker's goal that earned a depleted Cheltenham side a 1-0 win at Ashton United in the third round and he also scored twice in a 2-0 win over Yeovil Town on Boxing Day. One of his goals was the sweetest of strikes from a free-kick on the edge of the penalty area.

As well as their groundbreaking Trophy run, Cheltenham reached the third round of

the FA Cup for the first time since 1933/34. They held First Division club Reading to a 1-1 draw at Whaddon Road to earn a replay at Elm Park. Trevor Morley gave Reading the lead, but Walker hit an equaliser as Cheltenham put up a great fight, eventually succumbing to a late Martyn Booty goal. Walker made 34 starts and scored 8 goals during his first season with Cheltenham and won a Conference runners-up medal as Cheltenham finished second to Halifax Town to record the best finish in the club's history.

Walker had two aims the following season: to become the first player to score 100 goals in both League and non-League football and to go one step better and win the Conference title. The season started with a defeat and two draws, but Walker showed his best form in Cheltenham colours to help Cotterill's team win seven games in a row. He managed to leave two Forest Green Rovers defenders on the floor just by moving his eyes in a 2-1 win at The Lawn that signalled the start of the winning run. Everything Walker touched seemed to turn to gold and he achieved his first objective against Barrow in a 4-1 Conference win at Whaddon Road. He made 22 starts, with a further 10 as a substitute during the 1998/99 season and scored 4 goals. The best of which was an extravagant free-kick in a 3-0 win over Southport at Whaddon Road. The ball was laid back to Walker and he casually flicked it up, juggled it a couple of times and sent a looping shot past Billy Stewart into the net.

Even the Southport players looked on in amazement as the genius Walker contrived a goal that only he could have scored. Cheltenham fought off nearest challengers Kettering Town and Rushden and Diamonds to take the title by four points. Walker sustained an achilles injury that hampered his involvement in the latter part of the season, but his two seasons at the club were one continuous success story.

He was released at the end of the 1998/99 season after 55 starts, 15 substitute appearances and 12 goals and after finally hanging up his boots, he can often be seen working as a pundit for Sky Sports. He turns out for Chelsea in Masters Football and he still has the ability to breeze past players with his trickery and turn of pace.

Tim Ward
Midfield, 1935-1937

Tim Ward is one of the most famous players ever to represent Cheltenham Town. The club have signed a number of former international players and top-level stars in the latter parts of their careers, but Ward is one of only two former Robins to progress to the full England squad; the other being Phil Bach, who went on to play for Sunderland and win one cap against Northern Ireland in 1899.

Brought up in London Road, Cheltenham, Ward joined the Robins as a fifteen-year-old in 1935 in the days when the team was managed by former Leicester City and Middlesbrough player George Carr. After a trial match, Ward began to turn out for the Cheltenham Town reserve team that competed in the Birmingham Combination. He made his senior debut against Newport County in a 4-3 win, operating at left half, where he was to play for the majority of his career. He scored one and made another during his first appearance, immediately catching the eye with his impressive performance. It was not long before Ward was attracting interest from the scouts of professional clubs and Leicester City made an approach, but he was too young and stayed at his home town club.

He was told by his full-time employers Lindner's Appliance Works that he would lose his job if he ever missed work for football again, but he attended a trial at Derby County, the team he had supported as a boy. He signed a contract with them and earned £4 in the summer, £4 in the winter and £6 if he progressed to the first team. He was told by his foreman that he had been sacked, but he said 'No I'm not, because I am leaving anyway, I'm going to be a professional footballer with Derby County,' and his full-time career was soon under way.

Cheltenham received £200 for Ward and he went on to establish himself at Derby and also play for Barnsley. He had to wait for his international chance due to the Second World War, but he earned two full England caps, against Belgium and Wales in 1948/49. During the war, Ward served as a Nursing Orderly with the 15th Scottish Division and his unit, the 153 Field Ambulance, was part of the Royal Army Medical Corps. All his training was geared to fitness and emergency treatment. He made the occasional appearance for the Rams during the curtailed wartime leagues. He took part in the D-Day landings and his unit fought through France and deep into Holland. His army activities meant that he was unable to play in the 1946 FA Cup final, when County defeated Charlton Athletic 4-1 at Wembley.

When his distinguished playing career came to an end, Ward managed Derby, Barnsley, Grimsby Town and Carlisle United. Ward passed away in January 1993, but he remains a local sporting hero of whom Cheltenham can be very proud. His son Andrew wrote a book about his father's life entitled *Armed With a Football*.

Dale Watkins

Striker, 1997-1999

Dale Watkins was a key member of Cheltenham's FA Trophy and Conference winning sides and will be remembered as one of the most lively and lethal strikers to wear the red and white stripes.

Born in Peterborough on 4 November 1971 of Welsh parents, Watkins was already renowned for his goalscoring prowess when Steve Cotterill paid Gloucester City £15,000 for his services in the summer of 1997. He started out as a trainee with hometown club Peterborough. He made 10 League appearances and a total of 30 first-team appearances for the Posh after two years as a trainee at Sheffield United. He played wide on the right in those days and was loaned out to Grimsby Town and Rotherham

United during his Blades days. He was released by Peterborough in 1991 and spent two months playing reserve-team football back at Rotherham. He then became a prolific scorer in non-League circles, most notably for Rushden & Diamonds.

He had dropped into the United Counties League with a team called Baker Perkins who have since disbanded. He then began his climb back up the ladder with Grantham Town, who he played for in the Southern League Midland Division in the 1992/93 season. He fired 16 goals in the first few months of that campaign, prompting Diamonds boss Roger Ashby to pay £6,000 for him. His goals helped the Nene Park outfit to the Beazer Homes Premier

Above: Dale Watkins dons an England shirt for the first time in a semi-professional international against Holland in 1998.

Opposite: Dale Watkins in action against Norwich City during the 1999 League Cup tie.

Division title in 1996. He scored against Chris Robinson's Cheltenham side that season in a 4-1 home win for the Diamonds after Robins' loan goalkeeper Nick Goodwin spilt a cross into his path. He scored more than 100 goals in three and a half seasons at Nene Park and won Southern League Midland and Premier Division Championship medals and reached the FA Trophy semi-finals for the first time.

He then played a major role in Gloucester's most successful campaign to date. The 1996/97 season saw them come to within a whisker of reaching the FA Trophy final at Wembley and winning promotion to the Conference. Watkins

was once again on target against Cheltenham, this time scoring twice in a rare win for the Tigers over their Gloucestershire rivals on Boxing Day 1996. The second of Watkins' strikes was one of the best goals scored against Cheltenham in years and gave City a 2-1 triumph at Meadow Park after Jamie Victory had given the Robins the lead. Unfortunately for the Tigers, a massive build-up of League fixtures meant they were forced to play three matches a week towards the end of the season and they finished empty handed, largely due to fatigue. As financial problems ensued, they could not afford to turn down Cheltenham's offer for

Above: Dale Watkins celebrates a Jason Eaton goal against Dover in the 1997/98 FA Trophy semi-final second leg.

Left: Watkins on the ball against Woking in a 3-2 Conference victory in August 1998.

Watkins. He returned from a holiday and was told by City boss Leroy Rosenior that he was joining Cheltenham. Cotterill had brought in a player who he thought could score goals in the Conference and Watkins did not disappoint.

Watkins, who worked as a driver for British Car Auctions, scored some vital and spectacular goals in his first season at Whaddon Road. He struck up a lethal partnership with Jason Eaton and the pair netted over 50 goals between them as Cheltenham surprised everyone on their return to non-League's upper echelon. He hit a brace at Aggborough to secure a shock 2-1 win for Cheltenham against Graham Allner's Kidderminster. He then scored from the penalty spot to give the Robins the lead against First Division Reading in their first FA Cup third round tie since the thirties.

Watkins' goals were also vital to the Robins' glorious run to Wembley in the FA Trophy and he scored six in the first two rounds. He netted four in the first round tie against Enfield including a hat-trick in the replay. He also found the net twice against his former club Rushden and Diamonds in round two. He went on to score in the semi-final second leg draw against Dover, which meant Cheltenham would be visiting the twin towers for the first time in their history. Watkins' fine form for Cheltenham was rewarded with a call-up to the England semi-professional side for the home fixture against Holland at Crawley's Broadfield Stadium. He partnered Neil Grayson in attack and was named as Man of the Match after a typically energetic display.

After such success in front of goal the previous year, Watkins endured a season of injuries in 1998/99, but still managed to find the net nine times. He had a pelvis problem, a double hernia and an ankle injury which restricted him to sixteen starts. He came on as a substitute in the England semi-pro match against Italy at Hayes as John Owens' side won 4-1. He missed out on further caps due to his run of bad luck with injuries. He scored 5 in 5 during the crucial Christmas period including another winner at Kidderminster in a narrow 1-0 victory. Cheltenham won promotion and Watkins was offered professional terms, which he accepted.

Unfortunately, Watkins only played in nine Division Three games for Cheltenham. He never seemed to recover fully from his injury problems of the previous season and faced a battle for a place in the side with new signing Hugh McAuley. He decided to drop back down into non-League football and moved to Kettering Town. He reached the final of the FA Trophy with the Poppies and also helped them gain promotion to the Conference one year after relegation to the Dr Marten's League. He appeared against Cheltenham for Kettering in the FA Cup first round tie in 2001/02. He was given a great reception by the travelling Cheltenham fans, who saw their team win 6-1.

Watkins was always entertaining to watch; he was exceptionally quick off the mark and was never afraid to try his luck from distance. He scored some memorable goals and it was a great shame that he did not give himself more time to adjust to full-time football. Now retired, Watkins rolled back the years with a wonderful long-range strike for the Cheltenham Town Legends XI, who took on the current Cheltenham Town XI to mark Jamie Victory's Testimonial in July 2006.

Kevin Willetts
Defender/midfield, 1985-1994

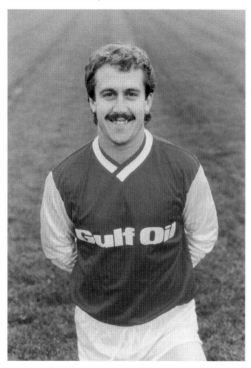

R obinswood-based Kevin Willetts was voted Player of the Year a record three times during his time at Cheltenham Town. Born on 15 August 1962, the versatile left-back or midfielder started out at Longlevens before stepping up to the Hellenic League with Sharpness. He was soon given a chance to impress by Robins boss John Murphy and made his full Cheltenham debut on 15 October 1985 and scored at both ends in a 3-3 draw at Wycombe Wanderers. He made 28 appearances during the 1985/86 season, before initially intending to return to Sharpness. But their manager at the time, former Robins' favourite Pat Casey, persuaded to him to give the higher level another chance and after returning to Whaddon Road, he remained there for nine seasons.

A plasterer by trade, 'Wilbur' as he was universally known, quickly established himself as a regular in the left-back role for Cheltenham as the club established themselves as a Conference club and reached the FA Trophy quarter-finals

for the first time in 1986. He made 46 appearances during the 1986/87 season and scored 1 goal in a 4-3 defeat to Gloucester City in a County Cup defeat at Whaddon Road. Playing alongside the likes of Brian Hughes and Ray Baverstock in defence, Willetts appeared in the 1986/87 FA Trophy last-eight tie against Kidderminster Harriers which attracted a crowd of 3,567 to Whaddon Road. Cheltenham lost 3-2 despite goals from Mark Boyland and a penalty from Hughes.

Willetts starred as Cheltenham reached the Trophy last eight again in 1987/88, where they were beaten 4-2 by Telford on 5 March 1998. Willetts also faced Wolverhampton Wanderers in the FA Cup first round when Brett Angell gave the Robins the lead, only for Wolves to hit five in reply, with future England international striker Steve Bull claiming three of them. Willetts made 45 appearances and scored 2 goals that season, before playing in 52 matches the following year and scoring another 2 goals. He then made 40 appearances and scored 7 goals during the 1989/90 campaign. He was ever-present in the 1990/91 season and featured in another big FA Cup first round tie – this time at Birmingham's St Andrews – where the Robins were narrowly beaten 1-0. During his Cheltenham career, Willetts won honours for the FA XI and the Middlesex Wanderers, touring Japan with the Wanderers during the summer of 1990. He made 48 appearances during the 1991/92 season which saw Cheltenham relegated from the Conference on the final day of the campaign. He scored a penalty in the final day win over Welling United, but it was not enough to save Cheltenham from the drop and they returned to the Southern League after seven seasons at the highest level of the non-League game.

Willetts made 42 appearances back in the Southern League, but joined Cheltenham's local rivals Gloucester City in February 1994 following a loan spell at Forest Green Rovers. His final starting appearance was a 3-2 defeat by Atherstone United on 16 October 1993 and he netted a total of 28 goals in 281 League

games for the Robins. He switched to Weston-super-Mare in August 1995 and was then signed by Graham Allner for Kidderminster Harriers. Willetts played some of the best football of his career despite his advancing years and helped Harriers to the Conference runners-up spot to Macclesfield Town in 1996/97.

Despite his sterling performances for Cheltenham, many onlookers believed that Willetts' talent was somewhat wasted at left-back. He looked more at home in midfield for Kiddy and contributed some vital goals during his spell at Aggborough. He appeared against Steve Cotterill's Cheltenham in 1997/98 as

the Robins and the Harriers renewed their old rivalries when Cheltenham returned to the Conference after a five-year absence. Willetts helped Harriers take Plymouth Argyle to an FA Cup first round replay in 1998/99 and joined Worcester City in June 1999, before reuniting with Brian Hughes at Witney Town as player coach in July 2000. He has since coached for Cheltenham Town's academy.

Willetts made a total of 367 starts for Cheltenham and a further fourteen as a substitute. He found the net an impressive 45 times for a player who played most of his games at Whaddon Road in the back four.

Mark Yates will be remembered as one of the most influential and hard-working players ever to represent Cheltenham Town Football Club. Birmingham-born Yates made his Cheltenham debut in a 2-0 Conference win at Southport on 30 January 1999. Steve Cotterill had swooped to sign Yates, then twenty-nine, from Kidderminster Harriers for £25,000. The Cheltenham team on Yates' debut was: S. Book; C. Banks, M. Freeman, R. Walker (B. Bloomer); M. Duff, L. Howells, M. Yates, D. Norton, J. Victory; J. Eaton (D. Watkins), N. Grayson (J. Brough). 'Yatesey', or 'Eddie' as he was sometimes known in reference to the Coronation Street character, was brought in to boost Cheltenham's Conference title challenge and provide some competition for places with the likes of Lee Howells, Bob Bloomer and David Norton.

By the end of the campaign, Cheltenham were celebrating promotion to the Football League and Yates was returning to the professional ranks after a five year absence. He had also been called up to the England Semi-Professional side for the internationals against Italy, Wales and the Highland League XI.

Yates was named in the centre of midfield for Cheltenham's first Football League match in August 1999 against Rochdale and he became a fixture in the starting line-up for the next four years. He was a model of consistency and only missed two League games in Cheltenham's first three years in the Football League. He played in 136 of Cheltenham's first 138 League fixtures. 'Staying clear of injuries was a great help,' Yates said. 'I didn't have a great deal of injuries in my career. It helps if you are enjoying your football as you tend to play better.'

Yates started his career as a trainee at Birmingham City in 1988 and he made 38 starts in the League for the Blues. Yates operated as a forward in those days and after making his debut as a seventeen-year-old during the 1987/88 campaign, he netted six goals in his time at St Andrews. He made his debut against Bradford City, going on as a substitute after ten minutes, but he was on the receiving end of an elbow to the head and needed stitches.

In 1991, Burnley paid £40,000 for Yates' services and he enjoyed some good times at Turf Moor. 'When I signed for Burnley, I knew straight away that it was the right club for me,' he explained. 'There was a great set of players there during the title-winning season and I had some very happy times. I bought my first house up there so I have some great memories of the place.' Yates left Burnley in 1993 after a loan spell at Lincoln City and with hindsight he believes that he made the wrong decision to leave:

In my second season, I didn't play as much as I would have liked. So, at the end of the 1992/93 season, when they offered me another year, I decided it was time to move on. Doncaster came in for me and I left, but it turned out to

Midfield powerhouse Mark Yates wearing the captain's armband.

be a bad move. I was young and just wanted to be playing, but looking back I think I should have stayed another year and seen how I got on.

After one season at Belle Vue, Yates temporarily left the Football League and signed for Conference club Kidderminster in August 1994. He made over 250 appearances for Harriers, many of them as captain. He helped Harriers finish as Conference runners-up to Macclesfield at the end of the 1996/97 season before making the move to Cheltenham in January 1999.

He won the Supporters' Player of the Year award in 2000/01 and he was one of the major players for Steve Cotterill's side as they adapted to life among the elite ninety-two clubs in the country. He was given the chance to face one of his former clubs in 2002, as Cheltenham took on Stan Ternent's Burnley at Whaddon Road in the FA Cup fourth round. Yates was a key player as Cheltenham caused a major upset and knocked the First Division side out with a famous a 2-1 win, thanks to goals from Russell Milton and Julian Alsop. In the next round, he was given the chance to face the club he supported as a boy – West Brom – at the Hawthorns. The Premiership-bound Baggies claimed a narrow 1-0 win but Yates and Cheltenham did themselves proud in their groundbreaking tie.

One of the features of Yates' game was his incredible stamina and throughout his 240 appearances for Cheltenham, he was a real workhorse in the centre of midfield. His partnership with Lee Howells was one of the features of Cotterill's all-conquering side and the two seemed to enjoy playing together in the engine room. He hit 19 Football League goals for Cheltenham and not many of those were tap-ins. He hit a long range stunner at Carlisle in 2000, but he rates his spectacular left-foot volley against Halifax Town on March 2001 as his best for the club.

As well as his FA Cup exploits with Cheltenham, Yates was involved in Birmingham's Leyland Daf final win over Tranmere at Wembley in 1991. Yates recalled:

> It was fantastic. Of the 68,000 fans there, about eighty-five per cent of them were from Birmingham. We were 2-0 up and they pulled one back, but big John Gayle scored the winner with an overhead kick with ten minutes to go. It was probably the highlight of my playing career along with winning the Championship with Burnley and the two promotions with Cheltenham.

Due to the absence of club captain Chris Banks, Yates took the armband and was outstanding in the Robins' play-off final win over Rushden & Diamonds at the Millennium Stadium. After Banks' retirement, Yates proudly took over as skipper on a permanent basis. He made 34 starts for the Robins in what is now League One and, when Graham Allner was sacked, Yates took over the caretaker manager's role with Bob Bloomer and Chris Banks. The trio picked the team as Cheltenham produced a much improved performance against Cardiff City, despite eventually losing 2-1.

Following the appointment of Bobby Gould as boss, Yates fought his way back into the side and was a regular again until the end of 2003. December saw him score against one of his former clubs, Doncaster, in a 3-1 defeat. That match turned out to be his last starting appearance for the club. He lost his place to on-loan midfielder Karl Henry and decided that he was at an age when he wanted to be playing first-team football.

Steve Cotterill always said that Yates was a great character in the dressing room. He set a good example to the younger members of the squad, who had great respect for the model professional. When he first secured the signing of Yates, Cotterill warned that he was not a fancy player, but he more than made up for that in sheer guts and determination and Yates proved him right.

After leaving Cheltenham, Yates returned to Kidderminster and made 14 League appearances, scoring 2 goals towards the end of the 2003/04 season. He linked up with his former Robins' boss Cotterill at Burnley, taking the role of first-team coach and assistant manager at Turf Moor. He then accepted his first managerial role at Conference outfit Kidderminster during the 2005/06 season.

If you are interested in purchasing other books published by Stadia, or in case you have difficulty finding any Stadia books in your local bookshop, you can also place orders directly through the Tempus Publishing website
www.tempus-publishing.com